The School Le⟨...⟩
Deserve

The School Leaders Our Children Deserve

SEVEN KEYS TO EQUITY, SOCIAL JUSTICE, AND SCHOOL REFORM

George Theoharis

Teachers College, Columbia University
New York and London

Published by Teachers College Press, 1234 Amsterdam Avenue, New York, NY 10027

Portions of the text and illustrations are adapted from the following publications: G. Theoharis, Disrupting injustice: Strategies public school principals use to advance social justice, *Teachers College Record* (in press); G. Theoharis, "At every turn": The resistance public school principals face in their pursuit of equity and justice, *Journal of School Leadership* (in press); G. Theoharis, Sustaining social justice: Strategies urban principals develop to advance justice and equity while facing resistance, *International Journal of Urban Educational Leadership* (in press); G. Theoharis, Woven in deeply: Identity and leadership of urban social justice principals, *Education and Urban Society*, *41*(1) (2008), 3–25; G. Theoharis, Social justice educational leaders and resistance: Toward a theory of social justice leadership, *Educational Administration Quarterly*, *43*(2) (2007), 221–258.

Library of Congress Cataloging-in-Publication Data

Theoharis, George.
   The school leaders our children deserve : seven keys to equity, social justice, and school reform / George Theoharis.
       p.   cm.
   Includes bibliographical references and index.
   ISBN 978-0-8077-4951-7 (pbk : alk. paper) — ISBN 978-0-8077-4952-4 (cloth : alk. paper)
   1. School improvement programs—United States.   2. Educational leadership—United States.   3. Educational equalization—United States.   4. Social justice—United States.
I. Title.

   LB2822.82.T53 2009
   371.200973—dc22

                                                                                    2008055468

ISBN 978-0-8077-4951-7 (paper)
ISBN 978-0-8077-4952-4 (cloth)

Printed on acid-free paper
Manufactured in the United States of America

16   15   14   8   7   6   5   4

To Ella, Sam, and Julie.

Contents

Acknowledgments

THIS BOOK is about justice and about what it takes to practice justice—belief in a better way, persistence and confidence to know it is attainable, humility to question oneself, and a spirit of collective action. Too often good leadership and even good books are looked upon as individual endeavors, not as collaborative works. This project stands in direct opposition to that idea—challenging the image of the lone principal or the solitary academic. Indeed, as I have learned from being a principal, from working with the principals discussed here, and also from writing the book itself, the best work stands side by side with and on the shoulders of a great many people. And thus it is a community of people that has enabled the completion of this work.

My first debt of gratitude is to the principals I worked with. In admiring their relentless pursuit of equity and commitment to creating communities of justice that have afforded thousands of children with the education they deserve, I have been inspired and strengthened by their triumphs, struggles, and leadership. They demonstrate what is possible and have broadened my view of what is attainable. My work now is to realize a hope that future principals will follow in their footsteps.

I am deeply appreciative of Brian Ellerbeck, Wendy Schwartz, and the team at Teachers College Press for their dedication in pushing my work to become both much deeper and simultaneously more accessible. I offer my sincere gratitude for their interest in producing a thoughtful book about leadership and social justice.

I will be forever indebted to Colleen Capper for her wisdom, insight, and steadfast devotion in moving the field of educational administration in the direction of justice. I have been blessed by her guidance and her unparalleled enthusiasm for my aspirations.

I extend my deepest thanks to Gerado Lopez, Deb Hoffman, Kelly Chandler-Olcott, Madeline Hafner, Sari Biklen, Kathleen Brown, Linda Skrla, Michael Apple, Paul Bredeson, Clif Conrad, Mary Louise Gomez, John Rogers, and Flo Hamrick for their guidance and analysis of how to shape and improve this work. I owe a great deal of appreciation to Tracy Davidson, Kathy Dempf-Aldrich, Ben Dotger, Jeff Mangram, Dee Sherb, Richard Shin, Julie Smith, and Ellen Tapley for their willingness to read and offer suggestions about my writing.

I want to thank Jim Scheurich not only for his career-long commitment to these issues, but also specifically for his piece "Highly Successful and Loving, Public Elementary Schools Populated Mainly by Low-SES Children of Color: Core Beliefs and Cultural Characteristics," published in 1998 in *Urban Education*. I first read this article during my principalship, and its documentation that other school leaders were dedicated to this work became a key part of "saving my sanity" as a principal.

I wish to thank Ruthanne Kurth-Schai for making the connection for me between public schools and enacting social justice. It was her inspiration that guided me into this field.

I will not name the numerous administrators, teachers, staff, families, and students from Frost Lake, Franklin, and Falk elementary schools who have allowed me into their hearts and lives. I do, however, wish to acknowledge their larger contributions to this work.

These acknowledgments would not be complete without my offering my appreciation and gratitude to my family, who have so deeply shaped my personal commitment to social justice and whose actions to create a more just and equitable world serve as inspiration for me personally and a reminder of the constant vigilance needed to enact social change. I want to thank my father, Athan, for his abundant pride in his son's scholarship, and my mom, Nancy, for her expectation that I bring a commitment to the common good in everything I do. I offer my most heartfelt appreciation to my sister, Jeanne, for her inexhaustible editing, selfless willingness to discuss and improve this work, and unwavering focus on crafting a more compelling message of social justice leadership. Thank you to Liz, Chris, Gail, Dodie, Jeff, Kris, Ammi, and Petra for ongoing support and encouragement.

This work would be significantly less interesting without an amazing support network that provided all kinds of rejuvenation and companionship to me. Thank you to my friends in Madison, Wisconsin, and my supportive community from "dear old Macalester." In addition, I feel renewed hope, from the network I craved as a principal, in my new community in the School of Education at Syracuse University—thank you for your work, your commitment to each and every child, and your ability to come together and celebrate.

Most important, it is difficult to express in words the inspiration and support that I have received from Julie Causton-Theoharis. Her passion for and practice of justice for people with disabilities deepened my own vision, and her imagination and dedication sustained me through my darkest moments. I cannot imagine the toll of the social justice principalship without Julie's support. Her persistent and joyful spirit kept me balanced throughout this book. Finally, to my daughter, Ella, and son, Sam, who provide real incentives to inject balance into my workaholic tendencies and whose boundless spirit has renewed my commitment to ensure our nation's promise of equity and justice for every child, and that all children have the school leaders they deserve.

Note on Methodology

I BEGAN this project while I was a principal of an urban public school. During my time as principal, my school adopted a completely inclusive service delivery system for students with special education needs and students learning English, tackled a range of curricular reform and staff development, wrestled with issues of race, and worked to create a climate where everyone (staff, students and families) felt they belonged—all changes that led to improved student achievement. However, the work needed to realize this took a serious toll on me emotionally, physically, and professionally. To sustain myself, I began to develop a small network of administrators with likeminded ideals to combat the void I felt of community and resources for school leaders committed to a social justice–oriented agenda.

At the end of my principalship, and while moving into higher education, I began this study to address that gap. While a rich literature had grown on social justice teaching, there was almost nothing that analyzed the work of actual principals bringing equity and justice to their schools. I sought out principals not only with these commitments, but who also had been successful in advancing them, using four criteria. They each (1) led a public school; (2) possessed a belief that promoting social justice was a driving force behind what brought him or her to a leadership position; (3) advocated, led, and kept at the center of his or her practice/vision issues of race, class, gender, language, disability, sexual orientation, and/or other historically marginalizing conditions; and (4) had evidence to show his or her work had produced a more just school.

Using purposeful and snowball sampling, I identified 18 principals, spanning three states, to participate in this project. Seven of the original 18 met the selection criteria; one of these ultimately chose not to participate, so that left six principals remaining to participate in and inform this project. In designing this project, I borrowed from the tradition of autoethnography (Cole & Knowles, 2001) and included myself, as a principal committed to equity and social justice, as a seventh principal for this project. In doing so, I combined a qualitative methodology with principles from autoethnography. Numerous scholars have used autoethnography as a methodological tool (Cole & Knowles, 2000; Dews & Law, 1995; Ellis, 2004; Jackson, 1995; Memeley & Young, 2005). Including myself

enabled me to make this work more personal and reflective. Tierney (1998) suggests that these are essential elements of meaningful scholarship—"a necessary
methodological device to move us toward newer understanding of reality, ourselves and truth" (p. 56). The principles of autoethnography and self-study that I
use for this project open my experiences to study in a critical, reflective manner.

Combining in one study an examination of my practices and experiences with
those of other principals provided for deeper and broader understanding of the
issues and strategies discussed. Having been a principal, I know that many current administrators rightly criticize higher education—and books about school
administration—as disconnected from "real schools." Simultaneously and yet
unfortunately, they often use this as an excuse not to submit their own experience
to analysis. Including my experiences within the group of seven is my attempt to
address both issues—realistic but still analytical. For me, studying social justice
principals and hiding my own experience would have felt disingenuous, incomplete, and inauthentic. My own experience indelibly influenced the kinds of questions I asked and what I looked for, how I understood the variety of challenges
school leaders faced, and how I understood the extent of possibilities that exist to
transform schools. I had begun my doctoral study before taking the job as a principal. When I returned to finish my degree afterwards, I saw the research very
differently. My experience led me to focus not only on the successes, but also on
how hard this work is, and on the strategies people employed to meet that struggle.

This project lasted over several years and included three to eight in-depth
interviews with each of the principals, a review of documents from their schools
(calendars, handbooks, meeting minutes, news articles, data charts, etc.), site visits,
discussions/interviews with school staff and families, a detailed field log, con-
vening the principals in small groups of two to four, and a group meeting of all
the principals. I had full access to the school and materials from my own experiences (including my personal calendar and journals), but I collected additional
data on my experience by completing interviews and site visits with the assistance
of another researcher. This researcher interviewed me in the same manner and
using the same interview protocols that I used with the other principals, but prob-
ing in ways she saw fit. Likewise, this researcher also completed site visits and
discussions with the staff/families at my school, which provided a set of data on
my experience that did not rely solely on my memory/perspective.

This book begins with the belief that social justice principaling is important
and needed. I had no intention of evaluating the caliber of social justice leadership, of comparing social justice principals with other principals in what they
achieved, or of defining which principals are the best. Accepting the premise that
social justice leadership is necessary, this study looks at what principals with this
drive who have achieved measurable success do—why they do it, the barriers they
face, and how they sustain themselves. With that in mind, by including myself, I
am not saying that my work as a principal was superior or inferior to others; rather,

I included my experience as another way to analyze and distill the practice of social justice school leadership.

In writing about the principals described in this book, I write in the third person, even when I am speaking of my own experiences. I used pseudonyms for the other principals and for myself (mine is Principle Tracy). I did this because I am only one in a group of equity-oriented principals. Describing myself in the first person would have exerted a particular power, shifting the focus to my experience, over the experiences of the group of principals. At a moment where school stories, from *Freedom Writers* to *Akeelah and the Bee*, draw big crowds, there was a danger that my narrative would grow too interesting. The seduction of the first person is that these narratives often get seen as the definitive answer or as the inspiring true story. Maintaining the third person throughout the text is necessarily awkward—it disallows that human interest identification, in a way that I hope leaves room for analysis and reflection.

Approaching the study in this way positioned my experiences as a part of this group and allowed for analysis across leaders and schools. Looking at seven school leaders provides a counterargument to the common belief that equity and social justice leadership are not possible, or are attributable to the work of one "great" or charismatic leader. While I began this project as a school principal, now as a professor of educational leadership, I come at this work from another necessity. The need for examples of school leaders who maintain a fierce commitment to issues of equity and social justice, for description of and reflection on what they achieved and the strategies they developed to do so, is critical to fulfillment of our nation's promise to provide the leaders our children deserve.

School Leadership and Social Justice

We can, whenever and wherever we choose, successfully teach all children whose schooling is of interest to us; we already know more than we need to do that; and whether or not we do it must finally depend on how we feel about the fact that we haven't so far.
—Ronald Edmonds, "Effective Schools for the Urban Poor"

EDMONDS'S (1979) call to educators presents a specific challenge to school leadership. At its core, this challenge recognizes that not only are schools failing many historically marginalized students but also the causes of that failure are known and remediable. Thus it is a matter of will and commitment, and not some sort of mysterious or elusive process, whether schools will change. In this book I examine principals who answered that call—who saw the host of ways injustice was being perpetuated in their schools, who chose to take up the challenge to ameliorate this, and who were able to make strides to alleviate the inequities. By highlighting the work and perspectives of seven principals, I provide a specific discussion of social justice leadership (SJL) grounded in the lives and words of principals committed to creating more just and equitable schools, in other words, the leadership needed to close the access, opportunity, and achievement gaps—leadership for social justice.

Uncomfortable with decades of unfulfilled promises to many students, the seven principals described herein demonstrated success not only with White middle-class and affluent students, but students from varied racial, socioeconomic, linguistic, ability, and cultural backgrounds. Three elementary and four secondary principals in the Midwest, these seven constituted a loose confederation of like-minded school leaders and met on a number of occasions to share stories and secrets, time-tested strategies for change, continued barriers to their work, and visions for the future. These seven principals, six of them White and one an Asian American, six straight and one an out lesbian, three women and four men, understood that creating a socially just school required looking at everything from playground upkeep to math tracking, from school discipline to the school office, to test scores. All worked at urban schools, but the demographics of their student

1

bodies ranged dramatically. One school was 99% African American, another 65% white, and the others a mix of native-born and immigrant students. Other than English, Spanish and Hmong were the predominant languages heard in four of these schools, with a smattering of Russian, Vietnamese, Turkish, and Mandarin sprinkled in. While many of the schools could have resembled juvenile detention facilities from the outside, inside the walls were covered with art and student work and the playgrounds had been brightened with colorful paint and new equipment. People entering the school could now be expected to be warmly greeted in the halls and in the office—and no obvious police presence was evident in these urban schools. These felt like schools you would want to be in—not escape from.

These seven principals had come to school leadership from markedly different routes (counseling, neighborhood grocery, education, music), had sharply divergent personalities (extroverted, pensive and unassuming, confrontational, diplomatic), and ran schools facing significantly different challenges. Three had been administrators for more than a decade, while the others were in the early years of their first principal job when they participated in this study. Yet all shared a number of values and practices. All believed that their schools had been failing many students and all knew their schools could do a lot better—that all students were capable of excellence and should be given an education befitting such tremendous potential. All seven were headstrong, often stubborn leaders who came to their schools with a vision for social justice. Yet all realized that schools only succeed through empowered teachers and all had built structures to promote democratic school governance. Painstakingly, they had built leadership teams of teachers, bringing together eager practitioners, committed to meeting the challenge of new practice, and resistant teachers, who had to be cajoled into any sort of change. All seven walked a fine line, critical of the practices of many of their teachers, while still always maintaining that their teachers were the professionals and were most qualified to determine the curriculum and instruction of the school.

These schools devoted hours and hours to professional development—not just the week before school or a day at Halloween but continuing over the years. And often much of the professional development would take place with the entire Staff working together—learning about and analyzing language development and exploring reading acquisition, inquiry-based math, the curriculum, and race. All these principals talked about race—a lot—with teachers and parents, among themselves, in administrative meetings, and in community settings. Refusing to accept that "kids are just mean," they did not believe that teasing or name-calling was unavoidable in their schools, and they sought to create an environment in which gay-baiting, racial, and gendered slurs were unacceptable in class, on the playground, or in the locker room.

The seven principals opened their offices daily to parents and teachers. They stood outside every day before school, walked the halls, supervised lunch, monitored the playground, played games with children at recess, and often could be found outside at the end of the day. They attended community meetings and invited parents for pizza in their offices. They visited and called students' homes. They knew that along with having good teachers, the best schools are deeply connected to families—but that many parents felt unwelcome or unsure of their place at school. It was the school's responsibility to bring parents to the table and so the principals labored to find ways to bring families into the school (through talent shows, health clinics, interpreter-facilitated report card conferences, community meetings, school-hosted wakes).

These principals did not hide from the data on their schools. In fact they talked about them; worried over the gaps in school performance along race, class and ability lines; knew the intricacies of their schools' statistics and spoke about them in public. They believed that facing the statistics was essential to the task of accountability and understood the pressures on school leaders to fudge these numbers, or obscure them, because real resources (not to mention public shame) were at stake—and could be lost. But they insisted on talking about it anyway. They were angry about the demands put on schools to fetishize test data as the only important indicator—and they resisted pressure to simply focus on these numbers. They shared many numbers, keeping track of students who had been disciplined or were missing school, of how many had health care and which ones came to school hungry, of how many were failing, of which parents came to school regularly and which seemed reticent, of grade patterns and individual reading levels. All posted significant test score achievements across *all* categories of students, yet fought to avoid the skill-and-drill and teaching to the test that had overtaken the district mandates and many neighboring schools. The process of accountability also necessitated changes in school discipline. Moving away from suspending students and warehousing "naughty" pupils in detention rooms, these schools embraced process-oriented forms of discipline whereby behavior was seen as communicative, students were expected to make amends for their action, and fresh starts were given. In doing so, they increased the amount of time students spent in school while doing away with many of the practices that had previously criminalized disruptive or truant students. Not only did they have fewer students with police records and fewer students suspended from school, they saw serious declines in negative student behavior.

Faced with increasing resource shortages, these principals voiced sustained objections to these shortages while at the same time wrangling money from superintendents and employing creative ways to maximize the money they were given. They held school carnivals and walkathons to raise money for a new playground or science equipment and frequently wrote to small and large entities (local businesses, federal department of education, and private foundations) to obtain more resources for their school. All moved their schools toward inclusive services. In all these schools, students with disabilities were educated with their peers; pull-out and self-contained rooms had been eliminated. A number of these schools had taught English-language learners in separate classrooms; this too was eliminated and these young people were supported in regular classes and learned English alongside their native-English-speaking peers.

All knew principals who had been dismissed for engendering the ire of parents, staff, or the central office and walked a delicate daily balance of promoting change, conversation, coalition, and confrontation. Faced with a phalanx of angry White active parents when the school detracked math, one principal had innumerable meetings with those parents, always making sure to include other historically quiet parents who supported the detracking and the teachers who had spearheaded this change. Another saw that most of the non-White parents did not participate in school activities and started a set of ethnic parent meetings—Black, Latino, and Hmong—that ultimately transformed the formerly-white Parent Teacher Organization and led to a vast majority of the families at the school participating regularly in the life of the school. Yet another, running a middle school, saw a troubling pattern of placement: When students of color and students with disabilities left his school and entered high school, the vast majority were not being placed in a foreign language class in ninth grade. With foreign language as a gatekeeper in terms of college admittance, this principal convened his staff to do something about it.

All were exhausted and had known periods of despair and nihilism in their years of work. They cried, they lost sleep, and their personal relationships suffered. One vomited every morning from feeling an overwhelming responsibility, and four sought out counseling for their exhaustion and despair. Through their struggles, however, they learned about themselves, established new ways to build supportive coalitions, and made time for rejuvenating their spirits. In the years since this group convened, two have left their principalship (one to higher education and one to retirement) and four have moved schools, but all continue to work to actualize the nation's promise to educate each and every child. This is an account of their work and ideas, the barriers they faced, and the strategies they developed.

BARRIERS TO SCHOOL SUCCESS

The principals discussed here worked to realize the nation's promise to all children within a larger context of political and social barriers. The landscape of inequality and inequity in the United States shaped the realities that these seven leaders experienced and that every public educator faces daily.

Poverty

One significant barrier schools face is the economic condition of the United States. Rapp (2002) reports that currently in the United States:

- Between 5% and 10% of the population has 95% of the wealth.
- Middle- and lower-income families are working longer, are more productive, but are earning less than they did in 1990.
- Employees have 4–6 weeks less vacation time than that of people in many other industrialized countries but are paid the same.

Further, Lyman and Villani (2002) state that according to the Children's Defense Fund, more than 12.1 million children live below the official poverty line, which is calculated based on 1950s patterns of homemaking and family spending that does not adequately account for today's economic realities, particularly the high cost of housing, which means many more children and families are poor whether or not they are officially counted. The Children's Defense Fund additionally reports that more than 9 million children do not have health insurance and the quality or lack of health care is a serious concern. Poverty, as well as lack of health care, pose a serious threat to a child's development, nutrition, early childhood educational activities, and achievement at school (Lyman & Villani, 2002; Payne, 1998). Indeed, at least 1 in 5 students come to school hungry.

Racism

While poverty affects all racial groups, Black and Latino families disproportionately face economic, health, and social challenges—more live in extreme poverty, median income lags behind that of White families, there is less access to health care, fewer pregnant mothers receive prenatal care, and many more boys will spend part of their life in prison. (Children's Defense Fund, 2005). Racism—notion of White privilege—is reflected in the often unquestioned and unseen norms of society (Delpit, 1995; Ladson-Billings, 1994; Singleton & Linton, 2006, Singleton & Noli, 2001).

The forms of discrimination described above are interwoven in the daily realities of the educational system. In studying the experience of students of color in public schools, Murray and Clark (1990) found eight manifestations of racism: insensitive or hostile acts by students and school staff toward students of color, biased application of harsh sanctions, inequalities in the amount of teacher attention given to students, biased curriculum materials, inequalities in the amount of instructional time provided, biased attitudes toward students, failure to hire educators and school staff of color, and a denial of racist actions by school staff. Many of these manifestations continue to exist today, as students of color have received more significant consequences for the same infractions as White students; Black and Latino students are often suspended for nebulous or attitudinal reasons as opposed to White students, who receive cut-and-dried punishments for drugs or weapons offenses; the teaching force does not reflect the racial and cultural diversity of students; and while progress has been made, culturally responsive curriculum, instruction, and discipline has not been truly embraced (Children's Defense Fund, 2005).

Differential Educational Opportunities

Racism, as reported by Murray and Clark (1990), is a significant factor contributing to the disparate achievement gap between students of color and their White peers (Delpit, 1995; Ferguson, 1998; Noli, 2002–2003; Singleton & Noli, 2001). This gap relegates many Black, Brown, Asian, and Native children to a second-class education and sentences them to a second-class future. Students of color and low-income students are overrepresented in remedial or lower-level classes, alternative schools, charter schools, and special education. This has produced disparate student achievement. For example, according to the Children's Defense Fund (2005), Black students and low-income students are twice as likely to be retained at least one time throughout their K–12 education, and students of color and low-income students are twice as likely as their White middle-class peers to be suspended. In New York State, while 79% of White fourth graders are performing at grade level, only 51% of Black and Latino students and 54% of low-income students are at grade level (New York State Education Department, 2007). Clearly, race and income are connected to school experiences, access, and opportunity and consequently to student achievement, yet in traditional education circles there has been a tendency to see that as evidence of the difficulties inherent in educating these children, rather than the flaws of the educational practice itself.

Special Education. Race and income are also connected to issues surrounding special education. Students of color and students from low-income families are placed in special education at increased rates as compared to their White and middle-income peers (Carlson & Stephens, 1986; Carpenter, 1992; IDEA Local Implementation by Local Administrators Project & National Alliance of Black School Educators, 2002; Ogbu, 1987; Riester, Pursch, & Skrla, 2002; U.S. Department of Education, 2001). Following from the assumption that certain populations of students are more difficult to educate and thus must be removed from the regular school population, such overrepresentation has enormous consequences rooted in the historic marginalization of people with disabilities (Karagiannis, Stainback, & Stainback, 1996).

For years, students with disabilities have been segregated and denied opportunities to receive the same education as their nondisabled peers. Nearly 50% of students with emotional/behavioral disabilities drop out of school; within 3 years of leaving school, 70% of students with emotional and behavioral disorders will be arrested (U.S. Department of Education, 2001). Only 63% of students with specific learning disabilities and less than 50% of students with cognitive disabilities, autism, or multiple disabilities graduate from high school (U.S. Department of Education, 2001). In New York State, only 28% of students with disabilities are performing at grade level, and only 50% are educated within a regular education setting for the vast majority of the day. These statistics show an improvement over the previous 10 years, but clearly students with disabilities have received a second-class education and their achievement both at school and beyond has been thwarted.

English-Language Learners. In the past 30 years the number and percentage of English language learners (ELLs) in schools in the United States has risen significantly. The percentage of ELLs has grown from 9% of all students in 1979 to 19% in 2003. It has also been reported that the number of students who speak a language other than English at home has increased by 161% over the same period (National Center for Educational Statistics, 2005). Traditional programming for many of these students has involved removing them from regular education either for a number of years or for substantial periods of time each day. This practice of separately educating ELLs has produced neither academic achievement nor a sense of belonging for these students (Frattura & Capper, 2007; Thomas & Collier, 1997). In keeping with the context of the New York example, 23% of ELLs perform at a proficient level by the time they are scheduled to graduate high school and only 27% of those students graduate in 4 years. As with students with disabilities, the continued separate model of ELL education has resulted in inequitable levels of learning affecting school and post–K–12 futures.

Typical Responses to Disparate Opportunities. There is compelling evidence documenting disparities in opportunity and access as well as sufficient data attesting to the achievement gaps between students who have been historically and are currently marginalized in schools and their more privileged peers. Within this era of standards and accountability, there is increasing pressure to raise the achievement of all students. This pressure results in a host of programs and approaches intended to address those opportunities and achievement gaps. In response, school leaders often make knee-jerk decisions that support, implement, and defend programs, curricular reform, and policies that fly in the face of equity and justice. These efforts are causing a rise in segregated, remedial, or tracked programs; the use of retention; and an alphabet soup of separate or "special" programs that target certain students but never address the core teaching and learning in schools, access to that core, or the climate of the school. While these efforts may be well intentioned, many are repeating the disparate access and achievement outcomes of the past (Reese, 2005). In many ways the reaction to these external accountability pressures heightens the need for leadership that centers school reform around issues of equity, access, and creating a warm and engaging school climate.

SOCIAL JUSTICE LEADERSHIP AS AN EFFECTIVE
ALTERNATIVE TO SCHOOL-AS-USUAL

In the face of current realities and despite the struggles that they bring, there are schools that provide exemplary education to their students across areas of school climate, curriculum, instruction, and access. These schools observe significant levels of student achievement across all groups of students; students who have traditionally been excluded from the full benefits of an excellent public school education are thriving, "placing [their schools] in direct academic competition with what are considered the better Anglo-dominated schools" (Scheurich, 1998, p. 452). Despite historic, political, and educational barriers that stand in the way of such work, the accomplishments of these schools and their staff are remarkable in how they raised authentic levels of literacy, connected to families, and engaged teaching staffs in both committing to excellence for all students and learning the skills to realize that.

Researchers often define excluded students as marginalized. Lopez (2001) operationally defines the term *marginalized* as being "often used to describe people, voices, perspectives, identities, and phenomena that have been left out or 'excluded' from the center of dominant society" (p. 417). I use the term to describe individuals who have been labeled as "outsiders" (Lopez, 2001) because of race, class, gender, sexual orientation, language, or ability/disability.

Literature on Social Justice Leadership

A recurrent theme from these schools and from the literature on school change is that exemplary leadership helps both to create the necessity for change and to make change happen (Fullan, 1993, 2001; Grogan, 2002a, 2002b; Theoharis, 2007). More specifically, there are leaders at these schools where traditionally marginalized students are thriving and who come to administration with a commitment to focus their leadership on issues of equity and justice. These leaders have led the intentional transformations to create schools that oppose oppression and suffering by transforming them into models of equity and communities of justice. Scholars and administrators alike have called for "constructive models" (Marshall & Ward, 2004; Theoharis, 2007) of this kind of leadership. In other words, school leaders are interested in asking, What does leadership that transforms schools into more equitable and just places, with an attention to climate and achievement, accomplish? How do leaders achieve the transformation? What knowledge, skills, and dispositions are required? What barriers do leaders encounter? How do leaders sustain themselves and their work in light of the barriers?

A small but growing body of literature on social justice leadership has now emerged. Special issues in academic journals make up a significant portion of this literature (Grogan, 2002a, 2002b; Marshall, 2004; Normore, 2006, 2007; Shoho,

2006; Tillman, Brown, Campbell Jones, & Gonzalez, 2006). Several books and book chapters are also foundational (Frattura & Capper, 2007; Larson & Ovando, 2001; Larson & Murtadha, 2002; Marshall & Oliva, 2006; Pounder, Reitzug, & Young, 2002; Scheurich & Skrla, 2003). Theoretical works examine the meanings of and perspectives on social justice; practical ones discuss how university preparation programs can prepare future leaders to take up such a cause. Empirical studies (Maynes & Sarbit, 2000; Oakes, Quartz, Ryan, & Lipton, 2000; Riester et al., 2002; Scheurich, 1998; Touchton & Acker-Hocevar, 2001) detail the realities and various aspects of school administrators leading schools with elevated percentages of marginalized students achieving at high levels. These studies typically begin with schools that are successful at raising the achievement of marginalized students, and then turn to understanding the leaders of those schools. The schools are the unit of analysis in this research. This is clearly distinct from literature where the unit of analysis is the leader committed to social justice (as in this book). What is missing from this growing body of literature is a discussion and details of concrete models and real school leaders who live out a call to do social justice work (SJL) in public school. In this volume I seek to supplement the theoretical perspective on SJL and improving the achievement of marginalized students with analysis of the practical and daily work of principals and administrators in schools.

There is more written on social justice teaching than on SJL. The literature on social justice teaching focuses on teachers and even families/communities and barely considers the ways in which SJL is possible through school administration. While the social justice teaching work relates in many ways to the issues involved in SJL, much of this work sees and has experienced school administration as part of the problem facing this teaching. Additionally, more academic and popular writing focuses on teachers (their realities, struggles, and triumphs)—not all this work resonates with tenets of social justice. However, there is very little scholarly or popular writing on school principals, their realities, their struggles, and their triumphs. This book addresses that lack as well, in that it brings a lens of equity and social justice to the realities of principals.

Defining Social Justice Leadership for This Book

It is important to recognize that defining social justice is not straightforward; there are diverse perspectives on what social justice and SJL means. Thus, this discussion of social justice and SJL begins outside the realm of education and school leaders. Rawls (1971) provided a broad framework of social justice. He proposed that two tenets of social justice are grounded in the spirit of equality: (1) All people have rights, so justice requires equality of treatment of all people, and (2) equal opportunity, so justice requires that each and every person must have a fair or equal chance. Rawls went further to frame social justice beyond foundational notions of equality—while essential, they provide an incomplete framework for social justice. His framework included two more tenets grounded in the spirit of difference or diversity: (1) People are different, so justice requires regarding and treating people as individuals, and (2) in rectifying inequities favor or advantage should be given to more vulnerable and marginalized members of society. Rawls's understanding of social justice builds from the distinction (and tension) between equality and equity. While Rawls was not focused on educational systems, this framing of social justice and the tension between equity and equality provides a broad way to approach SJL.

Freire (1990) articulated the notion that educational systems produce and reproduce oppression. He proposed a challenge that the purpose of education and schooling must be to undo oppression and create schools, systems, and individuals that resist and liberate. Bringing this critical theory foundation to educational administration, Foster (1986) challenged the field of school leadership to focus on the inequities and power that schools create and reproduce. He argued that "leadership must be critically educative; it can not only look at the conditions in which we live, but it also must decide how to change them" (p. 185). While Foster did not refer specifically to social justice, his work informed the growing research on leadership and social justice, as he used similar theoretical underpinnings.

In examining this charge that justice and equity should be central tenets of education leadership, Bogotch (2002) concurred that "improving social justice is a challenge that rests in theory and in practice with educational leadership" (p. 139) and that "there can be no fixed or predictable meanings of social justice prior to actually engaging in educational leadership practices" (p. 153). He asserted that, regardless of specific visions of social justice, leadership is key in the ongoing struggle for greater social justice and that any educational reform effort grounded in social justice "must be deliberately and continuously reinvented and critiqued" (p. 154).

Marshall and Ward (2004) argued that many in the field of educational leadership center SJL on the equality aspects described by Rawls in that many believe that "social justice means simply ensuring that laws for individual rights are observed so that access to education services is available to children with disabilities, children who speak little or no English, children of color and other legally protected groups" (p. 534). They critique that position by arguing that SJL is certainly about equality and fulfilling laws but, in practice, it is about "creating a greater good for all individuals, [and] social justice can mean finding ways to 'fix' those with inequitable access" (p. 534).

Practically speaking, educational leadership scholars Scheurich and Skrla (2003) articulated that this means creating equitable and excellent schools:

> We are aiming to create schools in which virtually all students are learning at high academic levels. We are aiming for schools in which there are no persistent patterns of differences in academic success or treatment among students grouped by race, ethnicity, culture, neighborhood, income of parents, or home language. In other words, we are aiming to foster schools that literally serve each and every student really well. (p. 2)

Further, Marshall and Ward (2004) proposed that SJL builds upon instructional leadership and pushes educational administration to the next level. They argued that 10 years ago school administration needed to act in congruence with a focus on instructional leadership, which now needs to evolve into a "dedication to social justice" (p. 535). This means that SJL requires a major restructuring of schools. Dantley and Tillman (2006) centered SJL on restructuring and altering school policy, procedures, and day-to-day operations that "perpetuate social inequalities and marginalization due to race, class, gender, and other markers of otherness" (p. 19).

In addressing the marginalization of groups of students because of their "otherness," Frattura and Capper (2007) were emphatic that the "number one leadership characteristic" involved in SJL is that "leaders must believe in their core that students learn best when they are educated in heterogeneous educational settings, period. If the leader does not have that belief then nothing else matters."

In building upon these ways that social justice and SJL have been described, I define SJL to mean that the principals highlighted here kept at the center of their practice and vision issues of race, class, gender, disability, sexual orientation, and other historically marginalizing factors in the United States. This definition necessitates inclusive schooling practices for students with disabilities, ELLs, and other students who are traditionally segregated in schools. Frattura and Capper (2007), Sapon-Shevin (2003), and Theoharis (2007) described this essential connection between inclusion and social justice.

This definition also necessitates that SJL not be seen as a fixed or static position. It requires ongoing struggle, advocacy, and reflection (Bogotch, 2002). This definition embodies a particular stance on SJL. First, it forces the concerns and needs of marginalized students to the center of the education mission. Second, it stipulates that those needs and the needs of all students be addressed in inclusive settings with attention to creating and increasing access to the core teaching and curriculum in schools for each and every student in heterogeneous settings; improving teaching and curriculum; and creating a climate that fosters a sense of belonging for all members of the school community. I am certain that all scholars and public school practitioners neither agree with this definition nor subscribe to SJL. Nevertheless, it is essential to be clear about the position and perspective I am bringing to this subject. All the principals who are a part of this book shared this perspective, in their words and in their practice.

ORGANIZATION AND CONTENT OF THE BOOK

Because there are few examples of actual principals who are committed to and successful in creating more just schools (and consequently few clear visions of what such leadership would be), this book lays out three important features of SJL: a portrayal of how real school leaders seek, succeed, and continue to struggle to create more just and equitable schools, in particular for their marginalized students; a framework for understanding social justice leadership; and seven "keys" to social justice leadership to help leaders create better schools. The first feature—the portrayal of real school leaders—is embedded in each chapter through the experiences and words of seven leaders, selected, from three states, for their commitment to equity and social justice as school leaders and their ability to change their schools to better realize that vision. The individual leaders are described in greater detail in Chapter 2. The experiences and work of these leaders were explored by means of three to eight interviews with each principal; ongoing site visits and participant observations at their schools over several years; documents from each school (contracts, meeting minutes, newsletters); relevant state and federally reported data, including those on student achievement; and meetings with the principals' staff members and school families.

Turning to the second feature, the book provides a framework for understanding SJL (Figure 1.1). The components of the framework are discussed in detail in

Figure 1.1. Framework for social justice leadership.

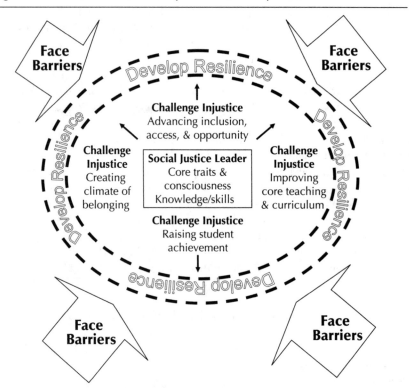

Chapters 2 through 9. I recognize that SJL is complex, messy, and not as straightforward as a framework of this nature implies with its distinct boxes and arrows. Yet I observed common aspects of all seven principals' beliefs and actions that were critical to their foundational beliefs in equity and justice and fundamental in their leadership.

The third feature, setting forth the defining attributes of such leaders, comprises seven "keys" to SJL:

Key 1. Acquire broad, reconceptualized consciousness/knowledge/skill base.
Key 2. Possess core leadership traits.
Key 3. Advance inclusion, access, and opportunity for all.
Key 4. Improve the core learning context—both the teaching and the curriculum.
Key 5. Create a climate of belonging.
Key 6. Raise student achievement.
Key 7. Sustain oneself professionally and personally.

These keys to SJL provide specific aspects of the complicated nature of how these leaders worked to close the access, opportunity, and achievement gaps. Each of the keys is embedded within specific components of the framework for SJL. These keys are not presented in numeric order throughout the book. For example, keys 3–7 are presented in Chapters 3–8, to provide a context for explaining keys 1 and 2, which is done in Chapter 9.

For the remainder of this chapter I describe the framework for SJL, component by component. As I do so, I illustrate how each of the seven keys fits within specific components of this framework. In the description of each component of the framework, I provide a brief description of the component, and then elaborate on any of the seven keys to SJL that pertains to that component. This framework and the embedded keys provide a structure for understanding principals who are committed to justice and equity, what they accomplish, the resistance they face, and how they sustain their work. I recognize that this is not the only way to understand or frame SJL, as there are multiple perspectives and stances on this work. This framework and the seven keys complement my operational definition of SJL and resonate with the words, experiences, and perspectives of these seven leaders.

A FRAMEWORK FOR SOCIAL JUSTICE LEADERSHIP

The Social Justice Leader

The leader her/himself is positioned as the center component of the framework for SJL. Chapter 2 introduces the principals that illustrate SJL as well as a starting place for building the center of the model: the social justice leader. Leadership is a personal endeavor and the educator who provides SJL is a central and vital aspect of this work. There are two keys in this component of the framework:

> *Key 1*. Acquire broad, reconceptualized consciousness/knowledge/skill base.
> *Key 2*. Possess core leadership traits.

These are described and illustrated in Chapter 9. I return to the center of the model near the end of the book, as these two keys are better explained after the other five.

Challenging Injustice

Moving outward from the center of the framework, the next component illustrates how SJL challenges injustice. While SJL seeks to advance an agenda more oriented toward equity and social justice, these principals framed their efforts around changing or challenging particular practices, ways of operating, and norms they encountered in their school communities. In many ways their efforts to create more just and equitable schools were enacted as they challenged injustice evident in their schools. The primary injustices they sought to challenge included structures that marginalize and segregate students and impede their learning, a deprofessionalized teaching staff and inadequate instruction, an unwelcoming school culture, and disparate and low student achievement. These principals worked to challenge the first injustice by advancing inclusion, access, and opportunity. They sought to change the second injustice by improving the core teaching and curriculum—a social justice instructional leadership stance. They addressed the third injustice by creating a climate of belonging. Finally, they confronted the fourth injustice by raising student achievement. The ways in which they challenged injustice provide four keys to SJL. Chapters 3 through 6 will move outward on the framework and focus on how these leaders challenge injustice:

> *Key 3*. Advance inclusion, access, and opportunity. Chapter 3 examines how these principals confront injustice by advancing inclusion, access, and opportunity for all (Key 3). The principals encountered multiple structures in their schools that separated, segregated, and denied marginalized students access and opportunity to a rich curriculum and instruction.
> *Key 4*. Improve the core learning context—both teaching and the curriculum. Chapter 4 explores how these principals improved the core learning context (Key 4) in their efforts to challenge injustice. When these principals began they found a deprofessionalized staff teaching an inadequate curriculum. These staff members were not treated as competent and capable professionals or allowed a voice in professional decision making. They found teachers who did not possess the necessary knowledge

and skills needed to reach all students and, in some cases, did not believe in the inclusive, social justice agenda the principals brought. These leaders encountered curricular programs that were insufficient and inappropriate. As the leaders worked to change that injustice, they *improved the core learning context.*

For the purposes of this book, the *core learning context* is used to describe the daily teaching and curriculum used in the general education classrooms but used by all staff, including general education teachers, special education teachers, ELL teachers, teaching assistants, special area teacher, and so on. For example, this would be the day-to-day curriculum and instruction in a general education second-grade classroom, or the pedagogical approaches and materials used in a high school general education science class. This includes the breadth of general education opportunities, among them art, music, and physical education.

Key 5. Create a climate of belonging. All seven principals found an unwelcoming school culture that created a disconnection between school and marginalized families/community and was not warm and welcoming to students, staff, or families. Chapter 5 describes how SJL changed that injustice by working to *create a climate of belonging* (Key 5). To do this they created a warm and welcoming school climate, fostered classroom community building, reached out intentionally to the community and marginalized families, and incorporated social responsibility into the school curriculum.

Key 6. Raise student achievement. These leaders felt a driving need to raise the achievement of all students but with particular attention to the achievement/achievement gap of marginalized students (students of color, students from low-income families, students with disabilities, and students learning English). While raising student achievement was a driving vision of their work, they rejected the often-used array of "quick fixes" or "scripted programs" and relied instead on the core beliefs that promote inclusion, access, and opportunity in an improved core teaching and curriculum, within an enhanced climate of belonging and causing an important impact on student outcomes. In other words, they did not use particular new strategies to "fix" student achievement but relied on the combination of all their other efforts and strategies in their work to change the injustice of disparate and low student achievement. Chapter 6 examines this sixth key and proposes a theory of socially just school reform.

Facing Barriers

Chapter 7 moves to the outside of the framework—*the barriers these leaders faced* in their efforts to challenge injustice. This chapter details that resistance and the impact it had on them both professionally and personally. In tackling injustice in the ways these principals did, they faced ongoing barriers that put serious constraints on SJL. These took a significant personal and professional toll on these leaders; the principals describe a substantial "cost" to doing this kind of work. While this component of the framework and Chapter 7 have no keys embedded in them, the barriers and their resulting toll are necessary components in understanding SJL.

Developing Resilience

Chapter 8 describes the last component of the model—the resilience the leaders developed:

> *Key 7.* Sustain oneself professionally and personally. The principals developed strategies to sustain themselves professionally and personally while challenging injustice in the face of their barriers. In order to sustain their social justice agenda to increase access and inclusion to the core teaching and curriculum in schools for each and every student in heterogeneous settings, improve that core teaching and curriculum, and fundamentally create a climate of belonging for all in the school community in the face of resistance, the leaders *developed a "ring" of resilience.* This ring is composed of both professional and personal strategies and constitutes an essential key to SJL.

CONCLUSION

In sum, the SJL framework has the social justice leader at the center. It is necessary to understand the core dispositions and knowledge/skills that the principals required. It expands outward to understand the ways in which the leaders worked to challenge injustice they encountered in their schools. Additionally, the framework includes the resistance they faced in their efforts to challenge injustice and views their work to challenge injustice as in direct conflict with the barriers they faced. At that contentious intersection, the principals developed strategies to advance justice in light of the barriers. These strategies are described as "developing resilience"—the final component of the framework.

The final chapter of this book provides future directions for practicing administrators and preparation of schools leaders. It positions equity and justice as not only desirable but also possible; not as a final destination but as an ongoing struggle. The book concludes with the distinction between SJL and traditional leadership—even traditional "good" and lauded leadership—illustrating how SJL works and explaining the distinction.

The field of "educational leadership does not have a history of being on the forefront when it comes to social justice" (Kohl as quoted in MacKinnon, 2000, p. 13). In light of this, and the recent 50th anniversary of the *Brown* decision, there is tremendous work to be done in creating schools in which each and every student thrives. It is imperative to seize this moment to commit our field, our research, and our practice to positioning educational leadership as a driving force toward social justice for marginalized students—the school leadership our children deserve.

The Seven Social Justice Principals
and Their Schools

I do this work because there are not enough other principals who deeply care about the kids from the margins and who can make equity and justice happen.

—Principal Meg

If I don't do this, who will?

—Principal Scott

I can't separate what is leadership and what is justice and equity work. It all has to be about social justice. There can be no separation.

—Principal Dale

THE SENTIMENTS expressed above are from principals who came to their positions with a desire to enact social justice, exemplifying leaders for social justice at a time when issues of SJL have attracted increasing numbers of school administrators' and scholars' interest. These real-life examples help to build the understanding that social justice in schools is not just educational theory or rhetoric but is actually practiced by leaders and *is* indeed possible.

This chapter begins with the center of the framework—the social justice leader. I introduce and describe each of the seven school principals whose work is drawn upon in this book. Who they are and why they do this work provides the essential context for understanding SJL.

INTRODUCING THE PRINCIPALS AND THEIR SCHOOLS

This work brings with it significant resistance to enacting a social justice agenda. Because SJL involves challenging entrenched norms within schools, districts, and communities, a sensitive discussion of this resistance is required. Thus I protected the principals' confidentiality by using pseudonyms. In the most sensitive situations I simply use the term "one principal."

Additionally, while understanding the local setting and particularities of the context where these principals work is appealing to both readers and me, the principals were adamant that their social justice work was *not* context specific. They felt that social justice can and must be enacted in every school. While there were important contextual factors at each school that they each considered, it was their experience that other leaders often used context as a reason not to engage in this kind of struggle. This chapter includes a general description of the group and, more specifically, the principals' paths and contributing factors that they attribute to their calling to SJL, how they approached their leadership, and some of the main challenges/issues they faced at their schools.

All seven principals worked in midsized to large urban public school districts in the Midwest. Three principals worked in elementary schools and four in secondary schools. The secondary principals were split evenly between middle and high school: There were two principals from each level. One principal was Asian and the other six were White; three were women and four were men. One principal was gay and out in the community and the other six identified themselves as straight. At the time I began studying their work, all seven had been public school administrators for at least 3 years. Their ages ranged from the early 30s to the mid-50s—three were in their 30s, two were in their 40s, and the remaining two were in their 50s. All seven principals had attended K–12 schools in the Midwest. Six had attended public schools from kindergarten through 12th grade, and one had attended a private Catholic grade school and then a public high school. Four graduated from suburban public high schools outside major midwestern cities. Two graduated from the public high school in their small town. One graduated from a large urban high school and later became its principal. These principals are referred to by the following pseudonyms: Principal Eli, Principal Taylor, Principal Dale, Principal Natalie, Principal Meg, Principal Scott, and Principal Tracy. Table 2.1 matches the principal to the demographic characteristics of their schools. The descriptions that follow of each principal's path to SJL in schools are in no particular order.

Principal Eli

Principal Eli grew up in a family that owned local, community-oriented grocery stores, shaping his commitment to community involvement in terms of being both active and responding to community needs. Eli described himself as a White Jewish male, though he stated he was not "very religious." He grew up in a neighborhood in a large urban area that changed from being predominantly White and significantly Jewish middle and working class to almost entirely African American and largely poor. He lives in the same neighborhood today. Both his family's grocery stores and the school he led were in that neighborhood.

Table 2.1. School demographics.

Principal	School Level	Total Students (N)	Students in Special Ed (%)	Students in Poverty (%)	ELL Students (%)	Students of Color (%)	Staff Experience	Staff of Color (%)
Eli	High	375	20	90	0	99	Mixed	67
Natalie	High	132	23	35	8	34	Mixed	15
Scott	Mid.	450	25	47	18	49	Mixed	13
Dale	Mid.	425	22	40	10	35	New	10
Meg	Elem.	360	6	25	16	38	Mixed	5
Tracy	Elem.	380	14	50	16	53	Veteran	8
Taylor	Elem.	290	8	8	14	34	Veteran	15

Notes: Adapted from Theoharis, 2004. Students in special ed = students with Individual Education Plans (IEPs) meeting IDEA disability criteria. This does not include students whose IEPs are only for speech and language. Students in poverty = students who qualify to receive free or reduced-price lunch. ELL students = students who meet state requirements for ELL services. Staff experience = ratio of newly certified teachers to veteran teachers; New = predominantly younger or newly certified teachers; Mixed = in general a balance of new and veteran teachers; Veteran = predominantly veteran/experienced teachers.

He started his professional career as a high school history teacher, but then left teaching to operate the family business, which he ran for 15 years. After selling the business he returned to work in public schools. He was an assistant principal for 2 years before he moved into a head principalship. Principal Eli attributed his leanings toward social justice work to not only running a small community-oriented and community-responsive business but also to the political climate of the 1960s and 1970s. When I began this project, Eli was in his 50s.

Principal Eli's path to school administration focused him on making school deeply connected with the community as a vital, positive force. He was compelled to become a school administrator because he felt many in "power" in schools were not interested in students' well-being or in creating schools where marginalized students where given "real-world" and "rigorous academic" opportunities. He felt a strong compunction to support and empower teachers in running an effective school. He brought this to a small high school that was being created out of a "mega-3,000-student high school." When Eli arrived, there had been significant levels of truancy, student fights, and fire alarms; 15% of students were passing state exams, and there was a 24% rate of the freshman cohort graduating in 5 years in this 99% African American community.

Principal Taylor

Principal Taylor was born in Vietnam and lived there until she was about 5. She fled with her family after the Vietnam War and lived on a boat off the coast of Malaysia for 2 or 3 months. Her family was sponsored by an uncle and moved to a large midwestern city in the United States. In leaving Vietnam, her family lost "everything"—status, money, land, and possessions. Taylor described this experience as quite a "hardship for her parents," who were always "adamant about a better life and an education" for their children. She attended public school in the United States, starting in kindergarten.

She attributed her personal commitment to social justice to her parents, the Catholic Church, and her family's experience of leaving Vietnam. These forces taught "me to do the right thing . . . that we're not here just for ourselves but for the good of everyone . . . [and] the whole idea of treating people with kindness and dignity." She began her career as a school counselor. That experience lasted 3 years and cemented in her mind the need to do equity and justice work as a school administrator. As a Vietnamese American principal, Taylor discussed her own racial identity as contributing to her ongoing resolve to deal with racial issues in school. However, she does not remember being a victim of discrimination as a public school student. Taylor spoke of becoming acutely aware of how community members, teachers, and other administrators enact their understandings of race toward her. She was in her 30s, never was an assistant principal, and was in her 3rd year as principal when the project began.

Principal Taylor's school leadership revolved around navigating issues of race, and how they affected students and staff by creating a marginalizing system, and issues of teacher empowerment. While she felt that teachers needed more analysis of issues of race and marginalization, they were trained professionals who knew how to nurture student growth. She brought these ideas to an urban elementary school in the "wealthiest part of the city." She indicated that there were relatively small percentages of marginalized students and that they were often "even more overlooked and disregarded" in that setting, because the general trends and tests scores of the school were not significantly affected by their low numbers. This school had an increasing percentage of ELL families, but was dominated by economically and educationally privileged White families who, in Taylor's mind, saw the marginalized students "as vastly inferior and less important" than their own children.

Principal Dale

When this project began, Principal Dale had been a principal for 16 years and was in his 50s. As one of the first in his family to go to college, he felt that his parents instilled in him the notion that "education was the route to a better life." Dale described his family as a major influence in fostering a sense of fairness and equitable treatment. As a White male growing up in a small town in the Midwest, he began developing his commitment to justice when he was an adolescent. Dale recalled what he described as an "awakening" in high school, when he first realized that some of his classmates were seen as "misfits" and thus excluded from leadership opportunities and the most rigorous academic experiences, as well as treated as of lesser value than other children.

He talked about his personal interest in history and how that allowed him to better understand discrimination, prejudice, and struggle. Labor history, Black history, and the relationship between the United States and Japan helped frame his commitment to equity and justice, which was intensified through his growing up in the 1960s and 1970s, living in a time of social change and unrest. He taught for 10 years in different positions in middle and high schools, became a gifted education coordinator for the school district for 6 years, never was an assistant principal, and then became a principal. He came to the principalship with a keen interest in creating a school climate in which students, staff, and families were treated well and enjoyed being part of the school. His driving focus was on creating equitable, rigorous opportunities for marginalized students—eliminating separate and pullout special education and tracking.

This path brought Principal Dale to a diverse middle school. When he arrived, this school was experiencing frequent student fights, significant police presence, a tracked academic program, and separate special education services. He felt that students of color and students with special needs were seen as second-class members of the school by many teachers and thus a lack of concern existed for their poor academic achievement.

Principal Natalie

Principal Natalie attributed her commitment to social justice work in part to a childhood within a very close rural family. She described her White, middle-class family as "pretty affluent" for the area. They were "always doing stuff for the community but not in a way that was pretentious, but in a way that they truly wanted to make things better." Natalie described her family as "instrumental in getting Title IX truly followed [at the local high school] . . . always doing these extra church things like going on mission trips . . . supporting other families," for example, when "a parent was dying of cancer. [As kids] we always saw that you are a part of something bigger than yourself." She hated high school and felt ostracized, which supported her conviction that no child should fall through the cracks in schools. She is a lesbian who is "out" at her school. Natalie remembered wrestling with and questioning her sexual orientation and how that contributed to her being cast out in high school. She felt "no support" from her school or community and only received "negative and confusing" messages about lesbians. Her personal struggles growing up and her interest in history contributed to her commitment to "leave things better than you came onto them."

She worked as the director for the YMCA and also for a nonprofit that worked with people with cognitive disabilities, and then took an administrative position at a technical school. Those experiences continued to shape her convictions to enact social justice by giving her a broader sense of community needs and how "fundamentally school could improve the lives of students both before they left high school and with community agencies while in school." Following those positions, she taught public elementary school physical education for 4 years and high school for 2 years. She became an athletic director and an assistant principal and had been a head principal for 5 years before she spoke of her experiences with me. Principal Natalie was in her 40s.

Her experiences drove her to be a principal who was focused on the students who were neglected in school and those whose lives were in crisis. While LGBT (lesbian, gay, bisexual, and transgender) issues were important to her, she focused on a broad conception of inclusion; her own experiences as a lesbian led her to create a school where all students felt valued and safe. She took that idea further: Not only was the school climate essential, but the students who traditionally were excluded or marginalized deserved a "rigorous, world-class academic" experience. She brought this leadership to a small high school that had previously been seen as "a joke school." With rapidly growing diversity, when she arrived her school was a place where staff felt that students needed to be made to feel happy; their focus was not on academics. District officials told her that this high school was a place where "all the misfits and oddballs" went, to be kept amused, out of trouble, and out of the way and that no "real learning" was happening there or was particularly needed.

Principal Meg

Principal Meg's commitment to social justice developed at the end of college and when she started teaching. She noticed discrimination and developed a sense of fairness growing up as a White female in the suburban Midwest. She did not feel the need or call to take action until the beginning of her professional career.

Her study of philosophy as an undergraduate was a significant factor in the "logic" she saw in working for equity and justice. Meg's commitment to social justice came from the positive influences of her brother in his reinforcing a belief in being responsible in the world and community, her cooperating teacher when she student taught, and her own personal struggles growing up. She also credited her early teaching experiences as a White teacher in a Black school with predominantly African American staff as formative in her own social justice development. She taught at this elementary school in a large urban area for 4 years, then became a principal in another urban district. She was never an assistant principal.

She was in her 30s and had been a principal for 8 years when we sat down to discuss her background.

Principal Meg's primary drive was to ensure that students of color were given the same rich experiences as those of their more privileged white peers. She felt strongly that every teacher needed to take responsibility for each child's learning and that the numerous separate programs that existed pulled marginalized students away from the elementary classroom. She saw that in urban elementary schools this phenomenon allowed people to expect that "someone else was going to take care of teaching the most challenging kids to read, think, and do math." She had a no-nonsense approach toward young children and expected students to be nurtured and supported by classroom teachers. She brought this conviction to an elementary school with a host of separate programs (remedial reading, English as a second language [ESL], various interventions, and so on) serving an increasingly diverse population of students. With a sizeable population of non-native-English-speaking families and families living in poverty, combined with a well-organized and historically vocal white middle- and upper-class "university faculty/pseudoliberal" community, Principal Meg faced pressures from many places.

Principal Scott

Principal Scott attributed his social justice development largely to his family's church as he was growing up. He was not active in this church anymore; he grew up with the Church of the Brethren, "a peace church similar to [that of the] Mennonites." He felt that the church exposed him to issues about the Vietnam War, social activism of the 1960s and 1970s, conscientious objectors, volunteer service workers, refugees, and issues of race. Scott, a White male, described an agitating moment in his early days of teaching that continued to propel him to do equity work.

> I started to see all the White kids in jazz band, no Black kids in jazz band, you know jazz is essentially invented by Black people and now the Black kids are not included in this particular activity in school . . . so I started to work harder at [changing] it.

Principal Scott started his educational career as a music teacher, though his undergraduate degree was in engineering. He received his license to teach music and taught middle and high school band and choir before becoming an administrator. His wife, family, and a community of "equity-oriented friends" motivated him to further justice and equity in his daily work. He was an assistant principal for 3 years. During this project Principal Scott was in his 40s and was in the 1st year as a head principal.

His path to school leadership brought a real commitment to the individual student who was struggling, combined with a macrolevel sense of how structural issues such as scheduling affected inequities at school. His main orientation that drove his SJL was navigating issues of race and how those played out in urban schools. When Principal Scott began at his middle school, the school was plagued with fights, in-school and out-of-school suspensions, a lot of racial and gay-baiting name-calling, and huge social and academic gaps between marginalized students and their peers.

Principal Tracy

As a White male in his 30s, Principal Tracy's commitment to social justice came largely from being a part of an activist family. Starting when he was young, he participated in social justice grassroots activism alongside his parents and sisters. "Being socially responsible and taking action to create a more just world" was a familial expectation.

He recognized that he was talented at working with children when he was in high school. As an undergraduate he made the connection between social justice and education. This combined what he saw as his talents with children with his drive to do social justice work. Tracy taught for 7 years in urban elementary schools, primarily in kindergarten and first grade, and was never an assistant principal. He had been a head principal for 3 years at the time this project began.

Tracy oriented his work around creating inclusive/integrated structures and access for students from marginalized backgrounds. He felt that a good elementary classroom, the breath of arts and special area curriculum, and hands-on higher-level thinking opportunities were best for all students—this extended from the classroom to after school programs. He was committed to making school a place that was warm, welcoming, and fun for students, staff, and families. This additionally meant democratic and open leadership practices and facilitating collaborative approaches to teaching. Tracy combined those with the conviction that many teachers had many misconceptions about marginalizing issues such as race, disability, poverty, and language.

He brought this to an elementary school that had seen dramatic demographic changes over the previous 20 years: A 95% White and middle-class enrollment had become one of predominantly students of color, 12 languages were now spoken, and 50% of the families lived in poverty. Many of the veteran teachers had not originally "signed up for working in the diverse school where they found themselves." As the diversity had increased, so had the proliferation of special remedial programs, pulling students out of the regular classroom. Tracy joked that when he arrived his school was a "pullout magnet school; if students have any sort of special need, we pull them out!" This school lacked such community resources as public health amenities, social workers, and housing counselors to assist with an increasing need. The school faced increasing levels of negative student behaviors, suspensions, and tardiness along with decreasing levels of staff morale. Fewer than half the students were achieving at grade level on state and local measures.

CONCLUSION

In looking across the experiences of these principals, four attributed at least part of their commitment to justice from their family's instilling in them a sense of social responsibility to the community—local or global. Three described the political era of the 1960s and 1970s as contributing to their beliefs about social justice and equity. Three felt that a personal struggle helped shape their commitment to justice. Three discussed a personal awakening about discrimination and inequity as shaping their own pursuit of justice. Three described their undergraduate studies as critical to their thinking about working for justice, and two principals shared that their church, in part, shaped this commitment. While there were similarities in what brought them to the social justice principalship, there was not one common path that led these leaders to seeking social justice through school administration.

CHAPTER 3

"There Is No Social Justice Without Inclusion": Advancing Inclusion, Access, and Opportunity for All

Inclusion is not about disability, nor is it only about schools. Inclusion is about social justice.

—Mara Sapon-Shevin, "Inclusion: A Matter of Social Justice"

A S THESE social justice leaders sought to reverse the injustice they saw and experienced in their schools, they worked to establish models of inclusion for all students. This chapter helps build an understanding of SJL by examining how principals committed to equity and justice created better educational environments for historically marginalized students. In doing so, they eliminated pull-out and self-contained programs for diverse learners (special ed, ESL, Title I, tracked math) and created inclusive and integrated services whereby children were taught in heterogeneous groups and received services from collaborative teams of professionals within the general education classroom.

Sapon-Shevin (2003) has challenged educational leaders to see inclusion in the broader context of social justice, not only as a placement or type of programming for students with disabilities. Heeding this challenge is complex and requires for many educators a new and expansive understanding of inclusive schooling. According to Sapon-Shevin (2003) as well as Frattura and Capper (2007), the work to achieve this broader understanding of inclusion must be central to SJL.

Numerous scholars (Frattura & Capper, 2007; Moses & Cobb, 2001; Oakes, 1985) report the damage and inequity of tracking and separate pull-out/self-contained programs for students with disabilities, ELL students, and students with other learning needs. The concept of inclusion is rooted in special education and serving students with disabilities. This complements the concept of integration, which is rooted in the civil rights struggle. While this is not a part of the Individual with Disabilities Education Act (IDEA), the recent reauthorizations of this law have moved toward giving preference to inclusive placements (Huefner, 2000), and the ability of schools to meet students' need in least restrictive environment (LRE) has grown dramatically (Villa & Thousand, 2005). However, it is important to see inclusive schooling in historical context, to examine the evolution of the special education inclusion movement and that of the education of other marginalized students.

Before 1975 and the passage of public law 94-142—The Education for All Handicapped Children's Act—students with disabilities were often denied public education or given an education in separate facilities and institutions. After PL 94-142, students with disabilities were often taught in groups of students with similar disabilities either within their home school district or in cooperatives among districts. The next step in this evolution was to bring students "home" and educate them in their home schools/districts, primarily in separate classrooms. This was followed by "mainstreaming" students with disabilities into general education for portions of the day, often without support, which led to the current and traditional notion of inclusion. The traditional understanding involves some students with disabilities being placed full time (the vast majority of their day) in general education. This often means overloading students with disabilities into a few classrooms or academic classes with one special education teacher and one or more assistant providing full-time support.

Looking across the history of the education of students of color in the United States from slavery to present day, it could be argued that students of color without disabilities have followed a similar, albeit distinct, path—from denial of education to segregated facilities to the move toward desegregation (Reese, 2005). It also could be argued that ELL students have had a similarly segregated path, and true language integration has never occurred. Despite sentiments to the contrary, real inclusion of students with and without disabilities has thus remained elusive.

The overlap of race, class, language, and disability has aided in preventing inclusive services for all students as schools have created a proliferation of programs aimed at students who struggle. This has resulted in an increased number of separate programs that have disproportionate density and numbers of students of color, students living in poverty, students learning English, and students with disabilities (Frattura & Capper, 2007).

This chapter focuses on how the social justice leader works to eliminate structures that marginalize/segregate students and impede their learning. I turn to the seven principals, introduced in Chapter 2, to illustrate one of the keys to social justice leadership:

Key 3. Advance inclusion, access, and opportunity for all.

Two aspects of this chapter make it distinct from the growing body of literature on leading for social justice, the literature on school improvement, and the literature on special education and leadership. First, there is minimal literature suggesting a connection between leadership for social justice and inclusive school-ing (Frattura & Capper, 2007; Sapon-Shevin, 2003, Theoharis, 2007 are notable exceptions) and more specifically there is little theoretical or practical literature about principals committed to social justice and how they ensure inclusive schooling practices for each and every student. Second, this chapter challenges the typical notion of inclusion and provides specific leadership examples of a new understanding of inclusive services that moves beyond some students being "in-cluded" and others not to systems that are poised to meet the academic and emo-tional needs of a diverse range of learners. The seven leaders discussed here moved beyond the traditional view of inclusion that assumed inclusion was a special education issue and that resulted in pushing some students with disabilities into typical classes with or without support. Moving beyond that traditional view, this chapter draws on these principals' view that inclusion is building services, col-laborative teams, climate, and instructional practices that give all students access, success, and a sense of belonging in general education.

In understanding how these leaders advanced inclusion, access, and op-portunity for all, it is important to note that they first articulated a vision that made an essential connection between social justice and inclusive services and also intentionally dismantled school structures that marginalized, segregated, and impeded achievement. This chapter begins with how the principals articu-lated the connection between social justice and inclusion and then describes the ways in which they created more inclusive schools for their marginalized students.

THE CONNECTION BETWEEN INCLUSION AND SOCIAL JUSTICE

In discussing their efforts to dismantle these excluding structures, the principals were clear about the connection they felt between social justice and inclusive ser-vices for traditionally marginalized students. The ways in which they articulated this connection provided insight on moving beyond the traditional view of inclu-sion. Principal Meg stated:

> We cannot pretend that our Black, Brown and poor kids are getting what they deserve when we remove them from the regular classroom. These students need more, not separate. . . . In removing the same students over and over we make them marginal community members. . . . Even with our best intentions to provide special programs for special ed, ESL, and Title I, these students are further segregated and receive a lesser educational experiences. . . . These students have the right to be in the regular class-room with the most skilled people in the school, their classroom teach-ers. . . . there is no social justice without inclusion.

Principal Natalie echoed this sentiment:

> When we remove students from their peers, time and time again the
> students who are taught in special programs receive watered-down
> academics. Also, and perhaps more importantly, socially we teach kids
> that separate is OK, and they do not need to work on getting along. The
> more we separate kids the less they learn to work together, understand
> each other, and get along. There is not equity or any greater good in those
> messages.

Principal Tracy shared a similar perspective:

> Look at who is in the programs that remove students from the regular
> classroom. There is a high percentage of students of color and low-income
> students in special ed, in the remedial reading program, in ESL. Where is
> the justice in the fact that the only kids who have consistent uninterrupted
> access to the core curriculum are White and predominantly middle class?
> We cannot in good conscience say that these pullout and separate pro-
> grams are better than the regular core and there is no evidence that these
> pullout and separate programs result in achievement. We are continuing to
> relegate the same students to the back of the education bus.

These principals are clear that in their leadership, they make a necessary connection between creating inclusive schools and social justice. While there are many
educators who believe in the idea of inclusion, these leaders saw it as a driving/
guiding philosophy for all their leadership. This connection drove them to take
action in eliminating what they saw as unjust structures.

STRATEGIES THAT ADVANCED INCLUSION, ACCESS, AND OPPORTUNITY FOR ALL

In getting rid of these structures the principals evoked four strategies to advance their
vision of a more inclusive and socially just school: eliminate pullout/separate programs, increase academic rigor and access to opportunities, increase student learning time, and increase accountability systems for the achievement of all students. The
principals placed the greatest urgency on the first strategy—eliminate pullout/segre-
gated programs. Thus, this strategy will be discussed first and in the greatest depth.

Eliminate Pullout and Separate Programs

The first strategy that these principals used to change structures that marginalize/
segregate students and impede their achievement involved restructuring the school

to eliminate pullout/separate programs. This restructuring meant that they moved to inclusive special education services, changed to inclusive ELL programming, detracked the math program, or did a combination of these. Teaching students in heterogeneous groups within the regular classroom was a critical philosophical decision made by these principals.

Principal Tracy. Principal Tracy worked with his staff to eliminate pullout and self-contained special education and ELL programs at his elementary school. The separate programs were replaced by "inclusive services provided within the context of the regular classroom through team planning and team teaching between special education/ELL teachers and general education teachers."

Before the restructuring, "80% of students receiving special education services were removed from their classrooms for instruction in resource rooms or self-contained special education classes." This instruction took place only with other students with special education labels. Likewise, before restructuring, "100% of ELL services provided to students also took place away from the regular classroom in a separate resource room without connections to their classroom or the general education curriculum." In examining the previous service plans with the staff, Principal Tracy showed that the daily schedule for the students with the most need was the most fragmented. "Students of color were being taken from their regular classrooms for ELL, special education services, and remedial reading, creating segregation throughout the school. For the most part, only the White students were not being pulled out of the classroom." Principal Tracy re-created a visual describing this phenomenon.

Figure 3.1 represents an elementary classroom and how different programs in Principal Tracy's school affected that classroom. The circles at the bottom represent the students in the classroom and are labeled to identify their race. The shapes at the top represent various staff members working in separate programs; the programs are labeled inside the shapes. Each shape represents an individual staff member; thus there are two special education triangles, as there were two separate special education teachers who worked with children in that class. The lines depict which students were removed from their classroom to go to which programs.

Figure 3.1 also shows which students by race received which pullout programs prior to Principal Tracy's restructuring. Tracy pointed out that some students were removed for different programs multiple times, creating a "very disrupted schedule" for these students and a "very disrupted classroom" for all. He also drew attention to the fact that with only one exception the only students who were never pulled out were White. "Clearly there were racist implications that needed to be examined and changed in how we were serving our kids . . . and with all those different people pulling kids out and all those kids coming and going, some kids multiple times a day, look at how impossible it would be to have any continuity of learning time or even extended time for reading or a block of time for projects, for the class as a whole but even more so for our marginalized kids."

Figure 3.1. Elementary classroom disrupted by the pullout services provided.

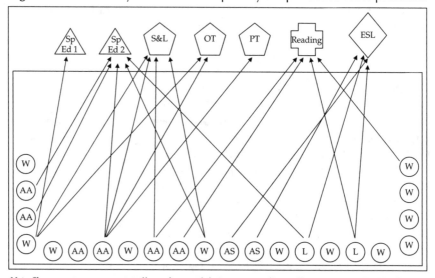

Note: Shapes on top represent staff members and their corresponding pullout programs: Sp Ed = Special ed teacher, S&L = Speech & language therapist, OT = Occupational therapist, PT = Physical therapist, Reading = Title I reading teacher, ESL = English as a Second Language teacher. Circles represent students and are labeled by the student's race/ethnicity: AA = African American, AS = Asian, L = Latino, W = white.

He also outlined the staffing patterns for the staff and showed that some special education teachers were working with seven or eight classroom teachers and the ESL teachers worked with about 14 teachers each. "This system prevented any meaningful teaming or collaboration around meeting the needs of students inclusively within the regular classroom." Figure 3.2 illustrates the special education service delivery for this school prior to the inclusive restructuring and Figure 3.3 illustrates the ESL service delivery prior to restructuring. In both Figures 3.2 and 3.3, the rectangles around the edge represent the general education classrooms, the ovals in the middle represent the various service providers in either special education or ESL, and the lines represent pulling students from their classroom to work with the service providers. In Figure 3.2, consider how some students are removed from their class, a few are included, and some have no access to the general education classroom. Also, consider the sheer number of classrooms from which some of the special education teachers were pulling students, the demands involved to connect with all those classroom teachers, and the impossibility of this service plan to foster collaboration between staff members as well as meaningful connections between students and the general curriculum. In Figure 3.3, examine the number of classrooms from which the ESL teachers were pull-

Figure 3.2. Special education service delivery prior to inclusive restructuring.

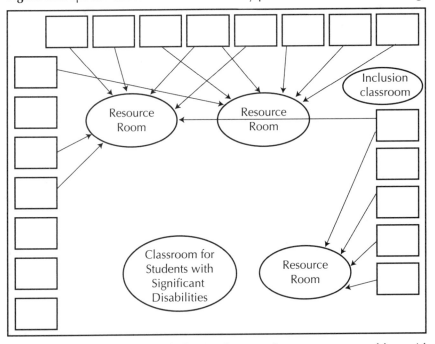

Notes: Rectangles = elementary general education classrooms. Resource rooms are used by special education teachers, who pull students from their general education classrooms. An inclusion classroom is one with 20 general education students and 10 special education students in which a general education teacher team teaches with a special education teacher. A classroom for students with significant disabilities is a self-contained special education classroom where all K–5 students who have significant disabilities receive their instruction and spend the majority of their school day.

ing students. In both cases, despite state and federal mandates that ESL and special education instruction be tied to the general education curriculum, the very nature of these service models made it impossible for the specialist to collaborate with classroom teachers and to make serious connections between the special programs (special education and ELL) and the general education curriculum.

Principal Tracy led a restructuring of the school to "create teams of teachers that met together to jointly take responsibility for the needs of all their students inside the classrooms. Special education teachers, classrooms teachers, and ELL teachers now work together to both plan and deliver their lessons." For example, teams at his school were configured in the following way: "two third-grade general education teachers, one special education teacher, and one assistant . . . or two fourth-grade general education teachers and one ELL teacher." After the restructuring,

Figure 3.3. English Language Learner service delivery prior to inclusive restructuring.

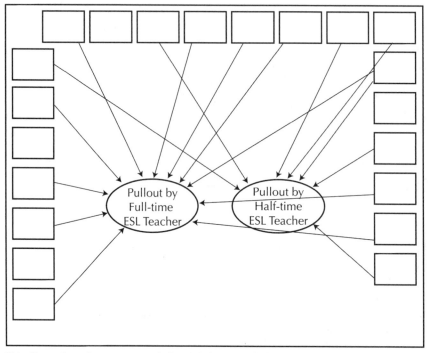

Notes: Rectangles = elementary general education classrooms. Pullout = ESL teacher taking ELL students to a ESL resource room to provide instruction.

> 95% of the students with special education needs received inclusive services and 100% of ESL services were provided inclusively. There were *no* self-contained special education rooms, no special education or ELL resource teachers who pulled kids out of their classroom to teach them. We had teams of specialists and general education teachers that worked together to address *all*, and I mean *each and every*, need present.

After the restructuring, teams were created across the school of general education teachers and specialists (special education and ESL teachers), as Principal Tracy described. The expectation was that the teams assumed collective responsibility for all students, as all human resources in the school were working on these teams, so there were no other separate programs to which to "send" struggling students. Further, the expectations were that all students received the education they needed through modifying, differentiating, and adapting curriculum and instruction—all students would participate in the general education curriculum with their peers. Principal Tracy pointed out that *all* meant *all*—students with severe disabilities, cognitive disabilities, autism, emotional disabilites, or minor learning disabilities and every other student in the school. This involved teams approaching teaching in new ways by letting go of old roles (general education teacher having sole responsibility of the curriculum and specialist having responsibility for students with special needs) and sharing ownership of all students and the curriculum. Moving in this direction required weekly co-planning and daily co-teaching and communication. This was built into the weekly schedule and was an expectation that necessitated teachers' changing how they worked. Initially, this co-planning felt like more work, as the teachers were used to planning alone, but as they evolved and teams developed, that feeling changed.

Figure 3.4 represents the service delivery model for special education after the restructuring; Figure 3.5 represents the service delivery for ESL. In examin-

Figure 3.4. Special education service delivery after restructuring.

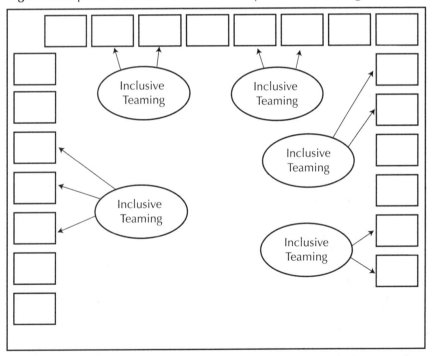

Notes: Rectangles = elementary general education classrooms. Ovals = special education teachers. Inclusive teaming = a special education teacher teaming with a general education teacher to meet the range of student needs within the classroom. Each special education teacher usually teams with two or three classroom teachers. Each team has one paraprofessional assigned as well.

Figure 3.5. English Language Learner service delivery after restructuring.

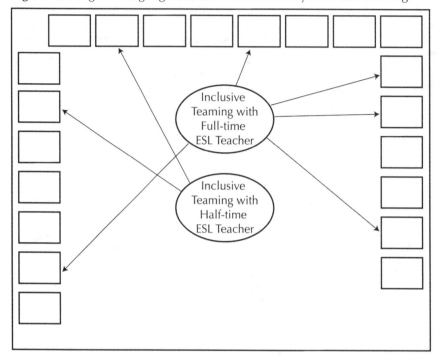

Notes: Rectangles = elementary general education classrooms. Inclusive teaming = a general education teacher and an ESL teacher collaborating and coteaching.

ing these figures, consider that students are no longer being pulled out to receive services and the specialists are working with significantly reduced numbers of classrooms. This model made it possible to expect collaboration within the general education classroom and curriculum because each specialist was paired with a smaller, manageable number of general education teachers.

This change in service delivery meant that special education assistants and bilingual resource assistants also provided inclusive programming for students. In addition, all talented and gifted as well as Title I reading resources were used to enhance the classroom learning inclusively through differentiation for students who needed diverse and extra challenges. The school went from having a segregated, pullout model to enacting a collaborative and inclusive model during Principal Tracy's tenure. While Tracy argued that creating a more inclusive school was a social justice end in and of itself, he also felt that these inclusive changes helped raise student achievement. These positive changes in student achievement are discussed in detail in Chapter 6.

Principal Meg. Principal Meg discussed her school's multiyear process to eliminate separate and pullout instructional programs. She recalled that when she came to this elementary school she spent time learning about the school, the staff, and the services. "During that learning process," she said, "I started really noticing how students who were in poverty or students in English as a Second Language or students of color in general were always being segregated from the regular education curriculum." She continued, "The traffic patterns were such that the Black kids go to Title I, the Brown kids go to ESL, the White kids are in the classroom, and the kids of color who qualify for more than one special program only get access to one because there wasn't enough time in the day to access what they were entitled to."

While questioning these patterns with her staff, Meg undertook a schoolwide needs assessment that involved staff and parents working together to identify areas of improvement. A call for smaller classes had come from all areas of the school improvement process; Principal Meg took that call for smaller classes, combined it with eliminating the segregated/pullout program at her school, and developed an inclusive model that resulted in using all her teacher allocations originally targeted for pullout special services (ESL teachers, Title I teachers, talented and gifted resource teachers, and discretionary allocation) to lower class size. The motivation was not only to lower class size, but also to get "more equity of time on task for kids, the least amount of transition for students, more research-based best practice, like eliminating pullout, and professional development for teachers to work with diverse populations of kids." A commitment to "using the knowledge and skills [of the classroom teachers] to try to provide a coherent instructional organized school day for the child who was the most needy" drove this restructuring.

Her effort resulted in inclusive service delivery whereby teachers learned the skills to meet the needs of all students in the classroom. There were no longer pullout ESL programs. Instead classroom teachers received training to gain dual certification in general elementary and ESL. There were no longer pullout Title I, or programs funded by talented/gifted and other local resources. Instead, classroom teachers had fewer students and provided all the literacy and other instruction for every child in their classroom. Special education services were already inclusive and continued to be provided collaboratively in the general classroom. Class size dropped from approximately 23 students in each classroom to 15, with no separate pullout programs. Principal Meg led these changes because it was "the best way to serve our students."

Principal Dale. Principal Dale relayed similar situations at his middle school. He spoke of two major initiatives to eliminate pullout and segregated programs. The first centered on the detracking of the math program. In his eliminating a tracked-by-ability math program, Principal Dale's thinking was that the previous lower-track and remedial-level classes for math were "populated by poor and minority students." He said, "We're trying to provide equity" by shifting to heterogeneously grouped math instruction.

Principal Dale's second initiative eliminated pullout and segregated programs "to pretty much fully include special education students into the curriculum. We have about 20 to 25% of our kids from special ed. They spend virtually all of their time in a regular education classroom now." This shift toward inclusive services encompassed students with all categories of disabilities, from mild to very complicated to significant behavioral challenges. The new configuration replaced the former service delivery system whereby instruction for the students with special education labels took place only in groups of students with special education labels, outside the regular education classrooms, in resource rooms or in special education classrooms.

The works of many scholars (Frattura & Capper, 2007; Moses & Cobb, 2001; Oakes, 1985) concur with the seven principals' work in eliminating pullout, segregated, and tracked programs. The purposeful connection these administrators made between inclusive service decisions and social justice aims makes an important contribution to understanding effective school leadership. Making this connection and then eliminating pullout and segregated programs thus becomes a critical component of the work of school leaders.

Increase Academic Rigor and Access to Opportunities

The second strategy these principals used to eliminate structures that marginalize/ segregate students and impede the latter's achievement involved increasing academic rigor in all students' classes, specifically for marginalized students, and providing access to broader school opportunities for marginalized students. Principal Natalie described the changes at her high school. "We moved from offering courses that only matched what teachers wanted to and were used to teaching, to a schoolwide process that looked at offering what any student would need to get into college." She saw a change in course offerings and an increase in rigor across all courses. "We have more academic rigor infused into the curriculum . . . and we are offering eight advanced level classes that were never offered before." She also talked about staff attitudes and how staff were used to having lower expectations about course content, and she noted that with a push for broader offerings she also pushed for higher expectations within the courses. "We used to just want kids to feel good about school, but now they feel good and we have 'big academics.'"

In his school, Principal Scott faced a different dilemma: Marginalized students were being forced out of programs such as fine arts. While this is not typically interpreted as academic rigor, the notion that these leaders were not compromising the breath of programming for marginalized students resonates with their commitment to access and broadly define rigor. Principal Scott discussed his restructuring of the middle school schedule so "all students had greater access to fine arts." He explained:

> Students often had to make the choice between [extra help in math] and taking band. This is a huge problem. . . . You see, my rich kids, many of them have music experiences outside of school, but for my poor students they need to have opportunities like band and the arts in school. They should not have to make the choice between math and music . . . so we had to change the way we scheduled students. It wasn't easy, but it was possible.

Principal Scott demonstrated how the lens of equity led to an examination of the broader school schedule and then modification of how the schedule was constructed. In his example, bringing this lens to the approach of scheduling helped create more access to arts across all student populations and thus a more equitable school program.

Principal Dale discussed detracking middle school math as an essential way to approach providing both rigor and greater opportunities. Not only does detracking increase inclusion for some students into the general education curriculum.

> [In addition, detracked math classes] give all kids access to higher-quality curriculum because most of the remedial classes don't work. . . . The curriculum is not challenging. . . . [Now], essentially, students are exposed to a broader base of mathematical work, moving away from what I would view as sort of arithmetic orientation, and giving kids opportunities to engage in more higher-level thinking.

He positioned increasing rigor and opportunities as a major driving force behind the changes he led to detrack math.

Principal Tracy echoed Principal Dale's beliefs about creating the inclusive services at his school that are described in the previous section on eliminating pullout and segregated programs. Tracy explained:

> What typically happens in separate programs like special ed, ESL, remedial reading programs, and others is that students do not have meaningful engagement with the general education core curriculum so it is no wonder these students fall and stay behind. School improvement for diverse learners is about giving all kids access to that core general education curriculum and then focusing all our efforts on making that core curriculum and instruction as good as possible. . . . Inclusion in this light is really about access and committing to all students their right to the core curriculum.

At both Principal Dale and Principal Tracy's schools, student achievement rose at the same time of implementation of inclusive/detracked classes. For example, students in special education improved from 13% reading at grade level to 60%, and all students improved from 50% at grade level to 86% at Principal Tracy's school. All the changes in achievement are discussed in detail in Chapter 6.

Principal Tracy also changed the structure of the elementary after-school program enrollment to give marginalized students greater access to important opportunities usually afforded to more privileged families who typically signed up early and filled the spots:

> The first-come-first-served traditional method of enrollment into our after-school programs continually excluded our students with the greatest needs. We created a lottery where we would take traditional enrollment forms but where we could also recruit the students who historically had been left out. So in our new system our most needy students had the same chance or better in enrollment as anyone else's. We also saved spots for students who needed the programs. And then when we talked with parents, I had a spot and could put them in the program at my discretion. . . . The programs were balanced; they weren't all high-need students and they weren't all privileged students. Each program was diverse and reflected the actual percentages of our school community. I didn't want one more example of how schools favor the White middle-class families.

Principal Tracy's example of changes in enrollment procedures transformed structures that denied marginalized students access to a wealth of opportunities.

This type of balanced and demographically representative enrollment is what Frattura and Capper (2007) called for in planning and developing all school services. Lyman and Villani (2002) suggested that students living in poverty are often given lower-quality programs, accompanied by lower expectations for their achievement. They argued against the belief that "schools can never overcome poverty's impact, that we should just settle for lesser learning, for lower academic achievement in high poverty schools" (p. 275). Their conclusion was consistent with the description here, in that these principals increased both rigor of academics and access to a wider breadth of opportunities. By doing so, they successfully worked to dismantle the "two-tier system" (Lyman & Villani, 2002, p. 251) that exists for marginalized students. Likewise, Scheurich (1998) found that the principals in the schools he studied also led their schools to develop high achievement "not by lowering expectations" but "by reconceptualizing what is possible for all children and by refusing any other result" (p. 461). His findings echoed the perspectives of the principals in this book in that holding high expectations for achievement requires a commitment to academic rigor for every student.

Increase Student-Learning Time

The third strategy that these principals used to change school structures to advance access and opportunity for all was increasing students' learning time. This took diverse forms, from reducing transitions during the school day to increasing attendance, from reducing out-of-school discipline to reducing dropouts. The principals saw these actions as central to increasing learning for their most marginalized students.

Principal Meg relayed a story about their elementary school restructuring. After eliminating the school's pullout services for ELL, Title I, and gifted and talented, she described what occurred:

> The kids had more continuity in their day; they had more time on task. All those transitions with students coming and going, all this time where students were walking to their "pullout" programs, all of those disruptions were eliminated. So basically they were getting more instruction while they were in school.

Meg believed that there were many benefits to eliminating the pullout services; one was that students receiving special services did not have so much downtime, so much wasted time walking to and from pullout classrooms, and so much disrupted time trying to transition between environments, which frequently led to behavior issues and more missed learning time.

Principal Dale sought to increase middle school student-learning time in two ways. First, he discussed the relationship he saw between learning time increasing as suspensions decreased. "Over the 7 years I have been here, we have had a 20% to 30% reduction in suspensions." Principal Dale stated that "this data means" that some of his "most needy students remained in school more days instead of being sent home." This happened because

> we developed relationships with kids, but additionally I changed the way discipline was handled and viewed. We moved from a "send the disruptive kids out of class and send them home" model to a much more relationship-based, process-oriented model. We needed to move away from a criminalization of our students to learning to see behavior as communication.

The second way he saw learning time increase was through a small but steady increase in the daily attendance rate of the students. "We worked to connect with our students, get our students engaged in class, and create classes where they felt they belonged and where they were challenged." Principal Dale went on, "The average daily attendance rate for our school 5 years ago was about 90% . . . and [now it has steadily risen] to 94%." Over the course of a school year a 4% increase means being in school, on average, 6 to 10 more days in school per student.

These principals' experiences suggested that an important aspect of socially just schools was a commitment to provide each child the right to the maximum amount of instructional time. The literature on leadership for social justice does not focus specifically on increasing the amount of learning time. However, the literature on literacy (Au, Carroll, & Scheu, 1997; Cunningham & Allington, 1994; Taylor, Pearson, Clark, & Walpole, 1999) and science and math (Burns, 1999; Moses & Cobb, 2001; Schmidt, 1997) has demonstrated this need for ample time during the school day for students to learn and apply skills. Hart and Bredeson (1996) argued that to positively influence student achievement, principals need to protect, maintain, and champion teaching and learning time. By increasing the learning time in their schools for marginalized students, these principals put into practice what the literature described as essential for high levels of student learning.

Increase Accountability for the Achievement of All Students

The fourth strategy the principals evoked to change unjust structures involved collecting and analyzing data to understand the academic performance of every student. Principal Natalie discussed the state of accountability and collection of information when she arrived at her high school as principal:

> Data wasn't kept before I got here. . . . Now we keep all kinds of data that we use to inform our decision making. . . . [We keep] the percentage [of students] who have been accepted to and plan on attending postsecondary . . . the percent of special education students . . . composite ACT scores . . . suspension data . . . AOD data . . . actual track of attendance data . . . and achievement data.

Principal Natalie took an additional approach to accountability in terms of student achievement. Until she became principal, the school "had never done a graduate survey. . . . I did a graduate survey and we got a lot of information from our graduates." She initiated an ongoing survey of their graduates, compiled this data, and used the information to drive planning for academic course offerings as well as improving the climate. "We needed to be more accountable to our students and their future after they leave us. Our graduate survey gives us information about areas of strength and areas needing change." Principal Natalie discussed the change that came from these surveys:

> Students indicated they felt connected to some of their teachers but not challenged enough and a number of students who were in college shared they did not have the same college preparation classes that their peers in

college did. So, this really helped our whole staff see the importance of adding more rigor and more college-levels courses for all of our students.

Principal Scott used his middle school achievement data to inform numerous conversations throughout the school. One example he cited entailed using data during difficult conversations with staff members. Before one such conversation, Principal Scott

> compiled a variety of data. I spoke with the teacher and brought up the fact that this teacher failed the most African American students in the entire school district. I had the data to show this, so we were able to have serious conversations about this serious issue.

Principal Scott stated that he felt using these data helped ground this and other important conversations in the achievement of marginalized students.

Principal Meg explained that when she arrived at her elementary school, there were no documentation or achievement records for any of the students learning English. When she discussed if ELL students were achieving at grade level, she stated:

> Well, we had no idea, if they were at grade level. It's sort of irrelevant because we didn't pay attention. So my guess would be that they weren't at grade level. . . . The biggest disparity was they weren't even counted or thought of like the rest of the kids at school. They're treated so separately and separate isn't equal so they totally get left out and so we'll say we're delivering these special service, but we're not going to pay attention to whether or not they're effective. Who monitors this? Nobody is accountable. When we started we had no data on our ELL kids.

Principal Meg explained that now every child at her school has informal portfolios and achievement data recorded at least three times a year. Local teachers designed the assessments, aligned them with state and local standards, and administered them individually or in small groups. A wealth of information came from the assessments and this information allowed the teachers to individualize their curriculum and design instruction tailored to the needs of all of their students.

These principals increased the level of monitoring of student achievement. While accountability is presently a politically charged concept and there is a caricature that people opposed to high-stakes testing deplore accountability, these principals present a different view. They were very pro-accountability and very pro-data. They used accountability not punitively but in a formative way. They demonstrated a commitment to understand the realities of their school and used data to help build that understanding for their teachers as well as for themselves.

Their desire to have and use data allowed them to lead discussions and planning around specific realities of their students, in particular their neediest students. The literature on leading for social justice complements this reality.

Riester, Pursch, and Skrla (2002) described how the principals and teachers in their study raised student achievement by using data:

> On-going data collection was a way to guide and inform instruction. . . . In these schools, data collection included the process of continually reviewing ongoing records of students' academic growth. The data took many forms. . . . Thus data served a multitude of purposes. (p. 298)

Scheurich (1998) noted that the principals and staffs he studied shared this ongoing commitment to using data. Scheurich and Skrla (2003) argued that data are

> highly useful for developing equitable and excellent schools. . . . We need a way to mark the student learning that we either are or are not accomplishing. In addition, when we have the kind of inequities by specific student groups, like racial groups, that we currently have, we need a way to mark those differences and to mark the erasure of those differences. (pp. 64–65)

Skrla, Scheurich, Garcia, and Nolly (2004) also describe the importance and use of data to understand where inequities in teacher quality, programs, and achievement exist. There were parallels between the principals they studied and the principals in this book in that they all shared a commitment to collect and use data to help improve the learning and climate of the schools in a more equitable fashion.

CONCLUSION

These seven principals used four strategies to eliminate unjust structures that impeded the achievement of all students. While the principals highlighted the first strategy of eliminating pullout/segregated programs as a necessary starting place, they were focused on advancing inclusion and access by using all four strategies. Combining them created structural improvements that made their schools more just and contributed to improved student achievement. They eliminated pullout/segregated programs, increased the rigor of academic classes and access to these opportunities, increased student learning time, and increased accountability for the achievement of all students. These changes are clearly distinct from what occurs in traditional school improvement, which typically focuses on adding new remedial or intervention programs or creates a new pre–special education referral system. These seven principals led their schools to change historically entrenched structures that brought marginalized students into more rigorous academic general education classrooms with support, eliminated pullout and separate programs, and increased access to opportunities outside traditional academic classes. Enacting these strategies had significant impact on marginalized students and their learning and improved the overall academic environment at all these schools.

The conclusion of this chapter will focus on the inclusive structures that the principals created and used as they eliminated pullout and segregated programs. The principals discussed here provided ideas about what the next generation of inclusion and integrated services will look like. Certainly, the placement of all students in heterogeneous classrooms where teams of educators collaboratively provide services for all students moves beyond the traditional model of inclusion of some students with disabilities to an approach that creates inclusive schools for all students. The examples provided by Principals Dale and Tracy whereby general educators and specialists co-plan, co-teach, and take joint responsibility for all students together articulate this next generation of inclusion.

Principal Meg pushes beyond even Principals Tracy and Dale with the restructuring of ELL services. This glimpse further down the inclusive and inherently socially just continuum relies on multiply certified educators with general education and specialist knowledge and skills who take sole responsibility for the education of a smaller number of students. Principal Meg pushes beyond restructuring to blur the distinction between general educator and specialist, positions responsibility for all forms of learning within the general classroom, and creates small communities of students so that teachers can actually reach each pupil. Regardless of their approach, the seven principals all felt and took responsibility for students with varying special needs—students in special education and ELL students. In contrast with many school leaders, these principals did not assume it was the special education director's role to ensure that students with disabilities got the appropriate education; they felt it was theirs. Nor did they relinquish the knowledge and authority about students with disabilities to the special education teachers; they knew all the students with disabilities in their schools and knew who was serving those students, and regardless of the district policies that brought students with special needs into their schools, these principals saw these traditionally marginalized students as equal to any other student in their school. The same outlook held true for ELL students. The principals provided specific approaches and broad philosophical concepts that can serve as a guide in developing more inclusive—meaning socially just—services for all learners.

In examining both the practices and success of these new models of inclusive services for all students, there are strategies and lessons to be learned that may benefit all students and, in particular, marginalized students, thereby demonstrating that social justice and inclusion are inherently linked. The aim of this leadership must be understood not as reaching a final destination of social justice, but as a continual struggle and process of striving for more inclusive and more socially just practices. These principals helped to define new evolutions of integrated/inclusive services that provide effective education for all students.

"Changing How We Teach, What We Teach, and How We Approach Schooling": Improving the Core Learning Context

In fact, [in numerous studies it was] found that nothing was as powerful as the quality of the teacher in predicting the achievement of children. Neither parents nor socio-economic status of the family were as powerful as good instruction in shaping the academic futures of students.
—Richard Allington, *What Really Matters for Struggling Readers*

A LLINGTON (2001) and other educators have argued that an essential component to improving student learning and creating greater equity in schools is ultimately the teaching and curriculum. While SJL must be centrally concerned about advancing inclusion, access, and opportunity, doing so alone is insufficient if the curriculum is inadequate and the teachers do not have the will or skills to reach each student. This chapter discusses how the seven principals worked to improve what they saw as an inadequate teaching and curriculum—another injustice imbedded in the framework introduced in Chapter 1. As described in Chapter 1, core learning context is used to describe the daily teaching and curriculum used in the general education classrooms but employed by all staff, including general education teachers, special education teachers, ELL teachers, teaching assistants, and special area teachers.

The principals described a number of components of this injustice. First, their teaching staffs, in general, did not possess the skills or will to reach every child. Also, when they arrived as principals in their schools, the principals felt that too many of the teachers had previously been treated as incompetent and not respected as professionals. Additionally, these principals felt that when they began at their schools the curriculum being used in many cases was outdated, incoherent, and far from what they knew to be acceptable. As these leaders addressed these instructional issues, they illustrated another key to SJL:

Key 4. Improve the core learning context—both the teaching and the curriculum.

The principals described here worked to improve the core by building staff capacity; recentering staff learning on equity and justice issues; adopting current curriculum approaches; and creating a climate that respected, appreciated, and empowered teaching professionals. This chapter begins with a discussion on how these principals articulated the connection between social justice and improving the core teaching and curriculum. It then describes the ways in which they approached this work.

THE CONNECTION BETWEEN IMPROVING THE CORE LEARNING CONTEXT AND SOCIAL JUSTICE

As these principals worked to change the reality they faced of a deprofessionalized staff and the inadequate teaching and curriculum, they made a strong connection between social justice and this work. Principal Natalie stated:

> What good are we doing these kids, the ones we have underserved for decades, if all we do is get them to school, include them, and be nice to them. We need to go beyond that. If we really believe school can make a difference for these kids, then when we get them here we have to really push them academically—they need and deserve big academics. This requires changing how we teach, what we teach, and how we approach schooling.

She was a strong advocate for traditionally marginalized students and felt that one way these students were continually underserved was through reduced academics.

Principal Scott also articulated this connection between improving the core learning context and social justice:

> We do not give all kids rich academic and nonacademic opportunities. The only way to really try to level the playing field is to give the kids who we have failed for years a better academic and extracurricular experience.

He explained that this requires rethinking "the curriculum we use" but also how "teachers and [teaching] assistants think about their kids and the instruction they deliver."

Like Principal Scott, Principal Tracy made this connection:

> It is not good enough to include students with disabilities and ELL students . . . in a mediocre education experience in the general education classroom. Upon our move to inclusive education, we needed to simultaneously address and improve what happens daily in that essential general education classroom.

He realized that a necessary complement to increasing access and opportunity for marginalized students was significantly improving the daily teaching and learning in the general education classroom.

Principal Taylor shared similar beliefs about rigorous academics, articulating a connection these leaders shared between improving the teaching and curriculum and challenging the norms of a deprofessionalized teaching staff.

> How can we expect teachers to really teach all kids if we continually treat them as incompetent? These are professionals in my building, they have their strengths and their weaknesses, but they are serious professionals who will not be able to reach our most struggling students if they are not valued and treated as capable professionals.

Principal Taylor believed that improving teaching and curriculum relies on a skilled group of staff who are treated as such. This was a key aspect to how these leaders understood the injustice of a deprofessionalized teaching staff. The seven principals believed that treating their teachers and staff members as professionals, through trusting staff expertise, establishing shared decision-making authority, not micromanaging, and holding expectations about ongoing learning and reaching all students was central to their efforts to improve the teaching and curriculum.

These principals clearly believed that improving the core learning context was a matter of social justice. Their beliefs, however, drove their actions as they sought to challenge the injustice of deprofessionalized teachers and an inadequate teaching and curriculum.

STRATEGIES TO IMPROVE THE CORE LEARNING CONTEXT— BOTH THE TEACHING AND THE CURRICULUM

These leaders saw a strong connection between social justice for both students and teachers and improving the teaching and curriculum. They used five primary strategies in this regard: address issues of race, provide ongoing staff development focused on building equity, hire and supervise through an equity lens, adopt common research-based curricular approaches, and empower staff. This combination of strategies pushed beyond the traditional, yet essential, aspects of instructional leadership. Using the seven principals, I again provide examples of the strategies to illustrate their work and reframe socially just instructional leadership.

Address Issues of Race

The first strategy these principals used to confront the injustice of inadequate teaching and curriculum involved addressing issues of race. All seven principals spent ongoing time with their staff discussing and learning about race. They conveyed a similar sentiment shared by Principal Taylor: "Engaging a predominantly White staff in serious, ongoing investigation of race is essential to building our ability to correct the racial injustices perpetuated daily in schools across this country." This involved informal and formal components. Principal Taylor described what she did at her elementary school: "Every staff meeting, a large chunk of time is now devoted to talking about race and equity issues." The following paragraphs give examples of what this looked like.

All seven principals led whole-staff conversations that examined personal beliefs and experiences with race. Engaging predominantly White staffs in discussing race was a key strategy in creating teaching staffs who moved beyond tolerance, beyond an understanding that race does not matter, to a place that valued diversity and examined the impact of race in the lives of everyone at school.

The principals used strategies to engage their staff in thinking about race. Five led activities with their staff that examined Whiteness and White privilege. Three led ongoing race discussion groups for staff. Four facilitated book groups using such sources as *"Why Are All the Black Kids Sitting Together in the Cafeteria?"* (Tatum, 1997), *Caucasia* (Senna, 1998), *Other People's Children* (Delpit, 1996), *From Rage to Hope* (Kuykendall, 1991), *No Excuses* (Carter, 2000), *Young, Gifted, and Black* (Perry, Steele, & Hilliard, 2003), and *A White Teacher Talks About Race* (Landsman, 2005). Two did this during staff meeting time so they could require the entire staff to participate.

Additionally, all seven principals planned staff development and facilitated spontaneous conversations about incidents that involved race. These conversations and planned activities provided a forum for staff to wrestle with the language and issues of race. The principals explained that the ongoing efforts around race were meant to foster changes in attitudes and behavior that consciously or unconsciously contributed to institutional racism and White privilege.

In addressing teachers' discomfort and inexperience with speaking and learning about race, five of the principals set ground rules for these conversations. A number of commonalities were evident across the ground rules. They isolated race from gender or socioeconomics in an effort to focus conversation about race and racial issues because they felt that many staff members' discomfort with discussing race led them to want to talk about poverty. In addition, they foreshadowed discomfort and nonclosure (Singleton & Linton, 2006) as a way to set the stage and remind their largely White staffs that these conversations and professional development were not going to produce, according to Principal Meg, a "neat and tidy package of racial epiphany or get us to some racial promised land. That this was going to be ongoing, messy, hard, and it wasn't going away." They did this during professional development and group discussions about race by reminding people this was an ongoing process, that they needed to wrestle with and sit with individual uncomfortable feelings, and that at the end of the session talking about racial issues would not be done. Finally, three of the principals used personal narratives and staff racial autobiographies as a way to keep race-based discussion and learning going and make race and privilege personal, local, and immediate (Singleton & Linton, 2006).

Additionally, all the principals infused race into their conversations about school data, such as student achievement, discipline, enrollment, and special education. Principal Scott described an example of this at his middle school:

> A year and a half ago, there were no Black kids in foreign language who have a disability, and there are White kids [with disabilities] who are. Foreign language is one gatekeeper for college, so there are no Black kids with an LD or ED label that ought to go to college? . . . We talked about strategies for how to fight against this.

Principal Scott brought issues of race into the ongoing conversations and meetings throughout the school day. While in one sense this conversation was about getting kids on track for college, it was also about making race a part of the daily thinking and language of schools. Bringing a lens of race into the daily practice of schools served to bring the needs of students who were previously relegated to the margins to the center of the discussion and practice.

None of these principals had schoolwide initiatives that tackled race, Whiteness, and privilege systematically with all students. However, by infusing race throughout their continuing formal meeting agendas, school improvement efforts and discussions with staff, the principals saw a new level of racial understanding *beginning* to develop in their staff. This new beginning of racial understanding did not translate into strategies for teaching reading or science, but led to a more reflective and caring approach to students of color. As Principal Meg described it, "Our focus on race did not change how we taught math, but it changed how teachers thought about their kids and how they treated them."

The seven principals felt that this kind of race-based learning was essential, because the preparation programs and professional development for many of their teachers, as well as their own, did not include this kind of reflective and intellectual work about race. Shields, Larocque, and Oberg (2002) and Rusch (2004) established that discussing and addressing issues of race is pivotal for schools in a diverse society. Shields et al. argued for establishing a community of difference and that such a community necessitates addressing issues of race and "begins, not with an assumption of shared norms, beliefs and values, but with the need for respect, dialogue, and understanding" (2002, p. 132). The principals discussed here attempted to meet the challenge put forth by these scholars in their work toward improving the core learning context. Principal Scott explained, "Purposeful and uncomfortable conversations and study about race certainly does not and has not changed our math or science curriculum, but it can change how we view, think about, and interact with our students, and this is a powerful implication." I position this strategy as an essential component in improving the core teaching and curriculum. While many articulate the need for ongoing learning about race, it was an essential aspect of SJL in their work as instructional leaders.

Provide Ongoing Staff Development Focused on Building Equity

The second strategy these principals used to improve the core learning context involved providing continuing staff development on equity gaps of concerns. These opportunities potentially provided their staff with greater skills to improve the curriculum and instruction for all students and, in particular, for traditionally marginalized students. While they each offered different kinds of learning opportunities, they all focused their staff development on aspects of the school with equity deficits.

Principals Natalie, Taylor, and Meg all remarked that they identified English-language learners as an underserved population in their schools. Principal Meg arranged for a local university professor to offer classes that would lead to English as a second language (ESL) teacher certification at her elementary school. In the restructuring described previously at Principal Meg's school, the new small-class-size model relied on dually certified teachers across general education and ESL. Principal Meg described this: "For our restructuring we were going to use our ESL allocation [the number of staff the district allowed/allocated Principal Meg's school for ESL, as well as other staffing allocation, discussed in Chapter 3] to drive down class size. This meant that I needed dually certified classroom teachers who could serve both roles at the same time." This required certifying numerous teachers across the school in ESL. She continued:

> We offered the ESL classes and got a [comprehensive school reform] grant to help offset the expenses for teachers wanting university credit for certification. While within a year or so, I had 8–9 teachers dually certified, over 25 staff took part in these courses—everyone from the evening custodian, to the office manager, from classroom teachers to art teachers, from [teaching] assistants to me.

Principal Meg realized that in order to meet the needs of her students learning English by eliminating pullout and segregated programs, her staff needed greater knowledge and skills about how to work with English-language learners (ELLs). She described the way she sought to fill that gap through professional learning. This learning filled a key need that would provide better education for a particular group of marginalized students. Principal Meg was creative in how she arranged this learning opportunity. She wrote and received a federal comprehensive school reform grant, which provided money to fund professional development. This arrangement with the university faculty meant that ongoing professional development became a university course; teachers could register, pay tuition, and receive university credit, or take the course and receive professional development credits through their school district. The federal grant helped to reduce the cost to teachers paying tuition.

Principal Tracy identified literacy as a large area needing improvement in particular for students of color, students of disabilities, ELL students, and students from low-income families at his elementary school. He focused staff development accordingly. He established "literacy as a priority for all staff: classroom teachers, special education teachers, ELL teachers, assistants, and reading teachers." In adopting a balanced literacy approach, he worked closely with a literacy coach to provide needed training for all staff members through courses, in-class modeling, and planning with teacher teams. Many staff enrolled in the after-school professional development, but Principal Tracy primarily expected the literacy coach to model in classrooms and help teachers change their daily practice. Eventually, he tailored the literacy coach's time to allow collaboration with teams of teachers during their planning "in order to change what happens day to day." Principal Tracy felt that

> the key to changing the way teachers taught reading was changing how they planned their daily lessons and schedule. The key was not holding more classes that teachers could sit in and ignore; the key was seeing the literacy coach model best practices right in their classroom and adapting their own daily plans accordingly.

Principal Tracy provided similar examples about focused staff development around the area of collaboration. He stated, "If we were going to have new inclusive structures and teams of general educators and special educators, the adults needed to learn to work together and adopt new roles." He planned and facilitated opportunities for staff to help them build relationships through learning effective ways for multiple adults to work together, plan together, and develop strong teams. He sought and received a grant from the district and state to provide a part-time collaboration facilitator to build, support, and develop teaching teams. He used staff development monies to pay for substitute teachers so teaching teams (special education and general education, or ESL and general education) had release time with a facilitator to co-plan units to meet a range of learner's needs. In his view,

> Being collaborative and inclusive were the expectations for everybody, but that does not happen because you want it to. Staff need time and staff development in changing their teaching from a solo act to a team effort. . . . That takes ongoing support and learning. Most teachers have not been trained to work this way, and co-teaching, co-planning, and sharing

responsibility requires adults working in new ways together, and that requires a lot of staff development.

Numerous researchers and school leaders (Darling-Hammond with Scanlan, 1992; Leithwood, 1994) agreed with these principals that a necessary precursor to school improvement and success was professional learning. This learning was focused on improvement goals, and the school leader played a major role in setting the course and tone for the school to continue learning. The principals followed those recommendations by arranging and facilitating focused professional learning for their staff. While this is not a new strategy to school improvement, it proved to be imperative to increasing student learning, particularly for marginalized students.

What is distinct about what these leaders discussed here is that they used their equity and social justice agenda to inform and guide the professional development. Not only the need to learn and use best practice, which most school improvement embraces, but also equity deficits drove the professional development. Skrla et al. (2004) suggest using formal equity audits to determine where improvement in equity is needed and then to address those areas. These principals, while not purposefully using such a tool, followed the ideas these scholars discussed on equitable leadership. The principals also saw that they advanced their social justice agenda through hiring and supervision.

Hire and Supervise Through an Equity Lens

The third strategy these principals used to promote justice in relation to the deprofessionalization of staff was to build staff capacity through hiring and supervising. The principals felt that bringing in the right people when staff openings arose helped build momentum in the direction they were leading the school. They discussed their belief that hiring was one important strategy to build a critical mass of staff who held similar beliefs about the principal's social justice agenda. Principal Meg discussed her use of hiring as a way to bring staff into her elementary school who possessed an inclusive philosophy and had experience, enthusiasm, and skills in issues of race and multicultural communities:

> When you put in the time and energy to finding the right people, it makes a huge difference because they share a commitment to the social justice and the inclusive direction we are going. Even one person can have a huge impact.

According to Principal Meg, an effective strategy was to "require all new classroom teachers to be dually certified, elementary and ESL. This fits with our inclusive ESL model and it means teachers come in with a great range of skills."

She felt that this not only brought in a wider breadth of skills, but also kept away people who were not interested in the inclusive nature of their restructuring. This was one way to build a mass of teachers who were interested in and had the skills to be the kind of teaching professional whom Principal Meg felt she needed. The principals positioned hiring and putting in time and energy into hiring as an important part of how to move forward in creating an overall staff committed to the vision of equity and justice.

While hiring did not necessarily give existing staff new skills, the momentum hiring created helped move the staff in a particular direction and in doing so increased the capacity of the entire staff to enact justice. By hiring people who had similar visions, these new staff members worked with their colleagues and shared new skills and ideas that also built staff capacity. This led directly to how these principals approached supervision.

The supervision that these principals enacted took two basic forms that moved the school in the direction of justice. First, they valued and trusted their staff. This resulted in their treating staff as professionals and not micromanaging their work. For example, they rejected the too-often-obsessive collection and review of daily or weekly lesson plans, they were present and active in classrooms, they found money or time to support staff who were "going above and beyond," and they used staff committees to make serious curriculum decisions. Second, in their own words, they were "aggressive" and "came down hard" when they found that staff members were failing to provide an equitable education to all students.

Both Principal Tracy and Principal Meg commented that they felt that valuing good staff and supporting them to become outstanding made up a part of their supervision plan. Principal Tracy believed that "treating people as competent professionals is key to supervision. I found staff are more likely to try new things or go along with some of my changes if they feel respected and not micromanaged." In speaking about supervising, Principal Meg remarked, "I search for ways to support the people who are doing great things. I try to make it easier on my teachers who are so invested in our toughest kids." These principals' convictions that a key aspect of supervision was about supporting, encouraging, and getting out of the way of excellent and capable staff became part of their daily approach.

Principal Meg also had times when she came down hard on staff who, it seemed, could not reach all students effectively. She monitored specific teachers' performance, organization, and curriculum when she found marginalized student behavior and learning needs not being addressed.

> I spent an enormous amount of time with [Mark]. . . . This teacher was popular with many families, but the Latino and Black students were never engaged, they were not engaged in reading, they were allowed to wander around. . . . We had weekly or biweekly meetings about his planning. I connected him formally with a couple of mentors and outstanding teach-

ers. I provided time for him to meet with, observe, be observed, have instruction modeled, and get feedback from these positive mentors . . . and we saw solid improvement.

Principal Meg felt that she had to make time for this kind of supervision in order to achieve the vision she had about education for her marginalized students. She felt it was a combination of being straightforward and blunt while providing meaningful support.

Principal Dale used what he called an "aggressive and humane combination" in terms of working to improve marginal middle school teachers. He sought not to ruin teacher's lives or pass marginal teachers on to other schools. In a number of cases, with support from both the teachers' union and Principal Dale, teachers who were not interested or perhaps not capable of working with a diverse population looked for and found a different career.

Additionally, all seven principals noted that their school staffs did not reflect the racial and ethnic diversity of their schools. While it is a national reality that the vast majority of teachers are White and female, three of the principals discussed how they had made some headway in hiring a more diverse staff than they found when they arrived. Principal Scott elaborated: "I've doubled the number of Black staff members in the school, actually tripled [it], seeing how there were two African American staff members in the school when I arrived and there are six now." He admitted that this was only one component of improving the middle school, an important one but not a silver bullet.

While the literature on leading for equity and social justice provided empirical evidence that marginalized students often have teachers who are comparatively less skilled and less qualified (Skrla et al., 2004; Touchton & Acker-Hocevar, 2001), the principals described here worked to change that reality in their schools. Although Scheurich and Skrla (2003) discussed the importance of high expectations, respect, culturally responsive teaching, loving and caring in the classroom, collaborative teaching environments, and continual development of content expertise, they centered this discussion largely in professional development and did not directly address either hiring or supervision. However, a growing body of research supported the notion that teacher quality has a dramatic impact on students' learning and improving their outcomes (Darling-Hammond, 1999; Pressley et al., 2001). Thus, the role of supervision with a social justice stance is critical to improving the education of marginalized students. The principals discussed here championed this belief through their hiring and supervision practices.

Adopt Common Research-Based Curricular Approaches

The fourth strategy employed to address an inadequate core learning context involved adopting common research-based curricular approaches for schools. The seven principals worked with their staffs to update and adopt new and common curriculum. While all seven principals knew that there were limits and guidelines imposed by the district office about the range of possible curricula and approaches to adopt, they were central instructional leaders in moving their schools toward current researched-based approaches. As Principal Natalie said, discussing her high school,

> No one had ever seemed to care that we did not have rigorous, inquiry lab science. It was OK to have some sit and get remedial science. So we changed that. . . . We adopted the same kinds of engaging, inquiry lab science found in other high schools' AP programs, but it was for anybody at our school.

It took time, effort, and some remodeling of the school space to create what Natalie called "a real lab space." Although she was relentless with district officials, she felt that this was a very slow process. She relied on a combination of harnessing district resources that were already committed for building maintenance with approaching local businesses to donate equipment and additional labor. For example, this meant having new, oftentimes donated equipment installed when the district electricians came to fix or upgrade other wiring, and at times having community members complete small jobs—sometimes under the table.

Principals Scott, Tracy, and Dale helped shepherd reform-based, constructivist math curricular approaches to their schools. This move was supported by their district administrations. Principal Dale explained this in regard to his middle school: "We know math is a gatekeeper and we know that tracking math is a bad idea, and math research also tells us that reform or standards-based math curriculums involve students in more equitable and mathematical thinking kinds of ways." They adopted a research-based, hands-on math curriculum across the school. Getting it off the ground required lots of professional development, conversations, and support. Principal Dale remarked, "There is always resistance to these reform-based math curriculums, and they are a real shift for some teachers, but it is better for students, and our math results have been steadily improving since." Principal Tracy echoed that sentiment and created a school team of representatives from each grade level at his elementary school to review, evaluate, and make a recommendation to adopt a common math curriculum.

> While it was clear that the way we were approaching math—everyone doing her own thing—was not working, the teachers needed to decide upon the new direction. Ultimately they picked the curriculum that the math specialist and I would have picked if I had made the decision, but I did not—it was their decision.

In this case the math specialist facilitated the process and helped to ask questions, but the representative group of teachers made the decision. Principal Tracy, working with the math specialist, created the process that helped the teachers make a decision, secured the resources to buy the curriculum, and ordered the materials, but this democratic process allowed the school to develop shared ownership of a new curriculum. Again, these principals approached school resources in creative ways. One strategy was to obtain permission to receive their percentage of the curriculum money the district was intending to spend on textbooks and take those funds to purchase the new math series and manipulatives.

Principals Meg and Tracy adopted a balanced literacy approach in their elementary schools. Principal Tracy described that when he started as principal, "everyone was doing his or her own thing with reading and writing. There were a lot of old basal readers and a lot of mishmash." Changing this required providing a good deal of professional development, everything from courses to coaching, from collaborative team discussions to action research projects, as well as securing and using monies to purchase the necessary materials to teach in this manner. This involved community fund-raising through the Parent Teacher Organization to buy trade books for a balance literacy book room and again the flexible use of district curriculum funding to maintain that. For example, one year Principal Tracy spent the entire amount of curriculum money he was able to get from the district to bolster the book room, which meant that for that year there was no money for other curriculum projects or materials. Principal Meg described some of the changes in curriculum she helped lead:

> We adopted a balanced literacy approach, like what Fountas and Pinnell [2001; Pinnell & Fountas, 1996], Keene and Zimmerman [2001] and Calkins [2000, 2003] describe. It was great and meaningful for students and teachers—many of [whom] were already skilled at this. I also set up training for the entire staff in direct instruction methods. This gave the teachers more and additional skills to use with all of their students.

Principal Meg was drawing on key literacy experts in the balanced literacy approach adopted, and she took another step in that she wanted her teachers to have the maximum range of skills possible, which is why she also provided professional development in direct instruction. She felt that this would help teachers reach more individual students within the structure of a balanced literacy classroom.

A key strategy to improving the teaching and curriculum in the principals' schools involved instructional leadership in adopting new, research-based common curricular approaches across their schools. To be clear, while all seven worked with their staffs to adopt common curricula and approaches across their schools, these changes were never imposed in a top-down manner, nor did any of these places adopt scripted or what one principal called "teacher proof" curricula. In many ways this is a central aspect of instructional leadership that many leaders and scholars describe. The principals took this strategy that is typical of good instructional leaders and combined it with the others described here to improve their schools and make them more equitable.

Empower Staff

The fifth strategy the principals used to improve the core learning context involved empowering staff. The principals were purposeful in ensuring that staff empowerment was a specific accomplishment in terms of advancing justice. This notion of empowerment is complex in that while the principals worked with staff in a democratic manner, including sharing decision making and developing a culture of trust and professional respect, the principals also maintained a strong vision and control of the big-picture agenda. Empowering staff was a social justice goal for these principals, as they held convictions about treating teachers and other staff members as skilled professionals. They maintained their own strong vision, they worked to build staff capacity and investment in their social justice aims, and they were adamant about empowering and respecting their staff.

The principals discussed implementing shared decision-making structures that created teams of staff to influence the direction and operation of the school. At most of their schools, previous leaders had taken two basic approaches. The first was controlling the information staff had: The principal would make big decisions and present them as done deals, but the process and background information necessary for staff to participate was never transparent. The second were shallow attempts at shared decision making or school improvement. This involved establishing teams that either made cursory recommendations that were often ignored by administration in the end, or were not allowed a say in the important matters of the school.

Principal Taylor discussed her commitment to the empowerment of her elementary teachers. She led a school that contained a group of "aggressive, organized, and politically savvy parents." She worked relentlessly to "protect" her teachers and "their ability to make the professional decisions" that she felt was their right.

> As the fourth- and fifth-grade teacher discussed detracking their math program, I knew this would be a very contentious change. . . . My staff made the decision. I was involved in the conversation, but ultimately they made the decision. . . . I felt this change, detracking math, in order to be successful needed to be a decision that professional teachers made, not a decision that I could make alone.

Principal Taylor talked about her conviction that this decision certainly should not be made by what she described as a loud group of "privileged and entitled parents."

> There was this aggressive group of parents, mostly affluent, with a feeling of entitlement. They did not like the detracked math program. They yelled and screamed and we had lots of meetings. While I value their ideas and we continue to work together, the curricular decisions of my school are the responsibility of the trained and skilled teachers who know this stuff day in and day out. These teachers made this decision in the best interest of all kids, not just the privileged ones.

Regarding keeping the professional decisions for her teachers protected from the privileged group of parents, she concluded that it is about "drawing the line." Principal Taylor felt that a segment of that group of parents was never supportive of the detracked math, but she did not overturn the decision the staff made to appease these parents. She also mentioned that some of these parents stopped complaining as they saw their children were being given a rigorous math experience.

Principal Tracy combined a shared decision-making structure with what he called "professional trust" to empower his staff. He described that structure:

> I developed a representative structure. Everybody in the school was on a team of colleagues of one sort or another: first grade, special areas, assistants . . . and that team picked a representative to this newly formed decision-making body. And we made a lot of decisions. I controlled the agenda, but we made a decision collectively in that group. I never went back on those decisions. That required a fair amount of trust in a democratic process and a belief that people make good decisions collectively. It gave ownership to more people.

Principal Natalie changed the structure of staff meetings and professional development, and now the teachers at her high school run all the meetings. She described the empowering structures and roles:

> The Monday meetings have always been more of a bitch session, or "you got to do this" or "you got to do that" and now I don't run them anymore. I have the staff run the meetings every Monday. The first Monday of the month is a business meeting where we talk about things we need to deal with for the school. The first 45 minutes of every staff meeting is used to talk about kids, kids that are struggling, so we try to find some ways to help them during that time. The last 45 minutes is business. The second

Monday of the month, the first 45 minutes is talking about kids that are struggling and what we can do to support them and then the last 45 minutes is staff development and that's where we work on the equity books. The third Monday, the first 45 minutes is always kids, and the last 45 minutes is committee work. The fourth Monday is, the first 45 is kids, and the last 45 is best practices. We share what each other are doing in their classes. I put together the agenda and the staff run them, and one staff will run the meeting, one staff will take minutes, everyone gets a chance to run a couple of meetings every year and that's made them feel more responsible for things instead of [their] telling me what I need to do to help a kid or what I need to do to change the school. The staff is making more decisions.

On the one hand, the principals brought a strong vision about what equity and justice could look like at their schools, but on the other, they showed that a key component to creating a more just and equitable school was to have empowered teachers making important decisions. In looking to the literature on leadership for equity and social justice, Riester et al. (2002) and Maynes and Sarbit (2000) described empowering staff as a key feature of creating more socially just schools. Since the principals in this book believed in their staff, they worked relentlessly to give staff a professional voice in their schools. This empowerment reflects what the growing body of literature on leadership for social justice supports: Staff empowerment is a lived priority.

In sum, strong connections can be made across the strategies of addressing race, providing staff development, hiring and supervising, adopting solid curriculum, and empowering staff that lead to more just schools. SJL recognizes the essential nature of building a quality and empowered staff that takes responsibility for the learning of every child and, in particular, the children who struggle the most. These principals combined a commitment to their staff with a fervent and unwavering vision of justice for the school. They neither led through top-down management style nor accepted a compromised vision while collaborating with staff. Both an autocratic style and a shared decision-making style—wherein everything, including the vision of the school, is decided collectively—are popular methods for school reform. These principals simultaneously rejected both and found their own hybrid through which they brought a strong vision of equity and justice and worked in democratic ways to achieve it.

CONCLUSION

The strategies discussed here are integral steps to replacing the inadequate teaching and curriculum that the principals found in their schools with a more professional teaching staff better able to reach each child and a rigorous curricular experience for all students—the fourth key to SJL, improving the core learning context. One issue affecting many of these strategies is the reality of school funding and resources. The leaders did not have a unified approach to dealing with funding challenges, but in looking across their experiences they tended to do two things. First, they leveraged the existing resources in new ways—used district building and grounds staff to help with new installations, reconfigured district curriculum funds to support yearly initiatives, or reconfigured staffing to support co-teaching or the offering of more advanced placement classes. Second, they invested time and energy in fund-raising through grants and community solicitations for specific initiatives.

The combination of these strategies moves beyond traditional instructional leadership with the inclusion of the equity and social justice lens that these leaders brought. This is most clearly seen in their tackling issues of race and focusing professional development around equity gaps, and in their commitment to empowering their staffs. The principals believed that these advancements with their staff not only created better teachers and other professionals, but began to build the foundation for changing the school culture/community.

The first two ways in which these leaders challenged injustice have increased inclusion, access, and opportunity, not to what they saw as a static inadequate general education, but to an improving teaching and curriculum. The work to improve the core learning context was not positioned as finite or complete, in that once they started addressing race and empowering staff, they were finished and the core was suddenly improved. These seven leaders saw this as ongoing and dynamic. They enacted an essential connection between their efforts to increase inclusion, access, and opportunities and their efforts to improve the core learning context. These were foundational aspects of creating more just and equitable schools, suggesting that challenging inadequate teaching and curriculum requires adopting a socially just instructional leadership stance.

While there is clear and abundant evidence that school administrators need to take on the role of instructional leaders, the work of these principals suggests that instructional leadership alone is insufficient—even within the domain of improving the core teaching and curriculum. This key to SJL—improving the core teaching and curriculum—is ultimately about bringing a lens of equity and justice to the role of instructional leadership.

"Connecting and Respecting": Creating a Climate of Belonging

*By building relations we create a source of love and personal pride and be-
longing that makes living in a chaotic world easier.*
                                        —Susan Lieberman, *New Traditions*

Individuals can resist injustice, but only community can do justice.
                                        —Jim Corbett, *The Sanctuary Church*

DEVELOPING AN authentic sense of belonging is central to developing socially just classrooms and schools (Kunc, 1992). With an increased focus on heightened accountability and improving test scores, less attention is paid to creating schools that students, staff, and families enjoy and in which they feel connected. While a key aspect of SJL is improving achievement (discussed in Chapter 6), the seven principals did not stress academic achievement or testing at the expense of creating schools that were warm and welcoming. However, when they arrived at their schools they encountered another injustice that they worked to change: an unwelcoming school culture—particularly for marginalized students and their families. This chapter focuses on how SJL worked to challenge that injustice—a part of the framework from Chapter 1—and presents the ways that these principals changed the unwelcoming school culture and altered the school discipline, which created a disconnect between the school and students as well as with community/marginalized families. This led to another key to SJL:

Key 5. Create a climate of belonging.

At its core, this chapter is about school discipline and student behavior. The notion of a climate of belonging reframes the traditional urban school discussion about discipline that has largely focused on safety and security. Safety and security concerns are symptoms of larger problems, not main issues in themselves. Seeing negative student behavior and safety as well as a disconnection between schools and families/community as fundamental issues of belonging is a complete paradigm shift in approaching school discipline. The seven principals operated from the perspective that a climate of belonging is an effective way to handle discipline and a holistic approach to creating more socially just schools. It is essential for readers to come to this chapter seeing the intimate connection between belonging and discipline as well as recognizing that this is a different discipline paradigm. In understanding how these leaders created a climate of belonging, it is important to recognize how they articulated a vision that made the vital connection between social justice and a warm and welcoming climate. This clear vision helped them to intentionally change the unwelcoming cultures that existed in their schools.

THE CONNECTION BETWEEN A CLIMATE OF BELONGING AND SOCIAL JUSTICE

The principals were driven to create a climate that authentically built strong connections between their school, students, staff, families, and community members and within these groups. In discussing their actions, the principals articulated the connection between social justice and a climate of belonging. Principal Eli remarked:

> The climate and tone we set makes all the difference. Typically, we send the message to kids and families that "we are the school, we do things our way, take it or leave it." But that just alienates them, and then we wonder why certain kids don't do well? We have to be human and really develop relationships with our kids and our neighborhood. Those relationships are how we get past the same kids getting the short end of the stick over and over.

Principal Eli pointed out that the climate of the school, perhaps more than anything, prevents or promotes access and learning. This positioned creating meaningful relationships and a welcoming climate as central to equitable and just schools.

Principal Dale conveyed the sentiment that all the leaders shared, that the climate of belonging was a powerful way to approach school discipline:

> We cannot forget that when we create schools where students feel connected, where they have adults they know care deeply about them, where they have a welcoming community of their peers, we are tackling discipline problems from a holistic approach. People think discipline is about punishment and consequences. Certainly everyone is accountable for their

own behavior, but discipline is really about connections between students, between adults and students, and between the school and students.

Principal Dale explains that a climate of belonging is not just fluff or a feel-good approach to school. It is an approach to school discipline that is often overlooked, shoved aside during tight schedules, and thought of as secondary to "real learning." Principal Meg expressed it this way:

> Inclusion is not only about the student with a disability being taught in the regular ed classroom. Inclusion is about how we treat all families, how we welcome all students, and how we value our teachers and staff. If we are serious about creating equitable schools, we cannot downplay the importance of connecting with and respecting students, families, and staff. If the way the school feels turns people off from the moment they enter the school, then what chance do we have that teachers will be motivated or able to reach students? What chance do we have that students will respect each other and deeply engage in learning? What chance do we have of developing two-way dialogue with families? Next to none. Without connecting people together and to the school, we will never close the achievement gap.

Clearly, Principal Meg acknowledged that without attention to meaningful connections between school stakeholders and without a climate that values and welcomes all students and their families, schools will perpetuate the achievement gap or remain inequitable and unjust. The leaders believed that a necessary component of changing unwelcoming and disconnecting school norms demanded fostering a climate of belonging.

STRATEGIES THAT CREATE A CLIMATE OF BELONGING

The seven principals worked to promote justice through their efforts to create a climate of belonging. Collectively, they used five strategies: build a warm and welcoming climate, foster community building in each classroom, reach out intentionally to the community and marginalized families, incorporate social responsibility into the school curriculum, and use a proactive and process approach to discipline.

Create a Warm and Welcoming School Climate

The seven principals worked to create a warm and welcoming climate. Principal Dale discussed changing how school personnel greeted families at their middle school to convey a sense of respect:

[When I began as principal] I saw many parents were not greeted warmly and parents were treated in infantilizing ways. The way the school welcomes parents can make a big difference. So I addressed how we needed to greet all parents and visitors. . . . This small step made a big difference. I can hear the difference, but more importantly, visitors comment on that difference.

Principal Dale helped frame respect and graciousness as key aspects of the tone that needed to be used by school staff to interact with all families. He worked with the main office staff and the entire staff on answering the phone, greeting all visitors, and interacting with students in the halls and office with a positive and friendly tone. It took time to model this and follow up on expectations. The framing translated into how students were seen and treated. Dale explained that the middle school had had a reputation for being a "wild place," but that reputation was changed, and parents' complaints about safety and order were significantly decreased. The change came about because "kids feel a strong sense of community. . . . I worked with staff to shift the focus at school from one of discipline and control to [one of] building relationships." Upon Principal Dale's arrival at the school, most students in special education had been in segregated classes and were not part of the schoolwide discipline system, but now students with disabilities were included in classes and in the discipline data. Even with that change, suspension and behavior referrals were reduced by more than 20%.

Principal Dale was convinced that through his emphasis on relationships with students, the climate changed. Police calls for behavior dropped by 60% to 70%, according to Dale. These changes, together with increased student achievement and academic rigor, reflected a less punitive and more accepting climate, in contrast to the "police state mentality that was prevalent here before." Dale operationalized the focus on relationships through how he and the staff greeted and treated students; his commitment to process-oriented discipline; and the stress on community building between staff, between students, and between students and staff. This changed the environment from one that approximated a "police state," fluctuating between chaos and martial law, to one in which hallways felt welcoming and the school a place that the children enjoyed. Parents and visitors were treated differently when they called or entered the building: A cold, almost "you are bothering us" manner became "Welcome, how can we help you." This required a persistent focus on modeling this, being clear about expectations, providing training in community building, and following up through supervision of the expectations.

Principal Taylor's philosophy was similar to that of the other principals, in that she felt that relationships with staff, students, and parents could help to transform the elementary school climate. She discussed how she also focused staff members to invest themselves in getting to know students:

I instituted weekly recognition of students. Each teacher nominated a number of students each week for individual accomplishments with the goal of every student being recognized multiple times a year. I gave out thousands of individual awards and the kids and staff loved it.

This changed the connection students had with their school, and while it is impossible to say that this led to fewer behavior problems, it is true that through an emphasis on belonging, negative behavior decreased. This activity was really about finding ways to acknowledge each student and find strengths and ways to appreciate students who would not have historically been recognized. Taylor also brought up the importance of staff appreciation:

I tried to establish norms for staff to appreciate each other. One way was to create time at staff meetings for staff to appreciate each other. Sometimes we did this in writing because then more people felt comfortable and more people were recognized. In 3 years we did hundreds and hundreds of written and verbal appreciations.

Furthermore, Principal Taylor acknowledged the "small steps" that can ultimately change the climate of a school. This was not about creating a recipe for building a positive culture, but rather about implementing small changes that reinforced the values of the principals' visions of equity and social justice.

At her high school, Principal Natalie fostered the development of a gay-straight alliance. She did not act as the advisor for this organization, but was an active supporter. She saw this as a necessary component to helping students who were lesbian, gay, bisexual, transgender, or questioning their sexuality have a safe community within the school.

Principal Tracy explained that the efforts to create a warmer and more welcoming climate took various forms at his elementary school. He encouraged and supported his staff—and in particular, the art teacher—to transform the inside of the building so that every hallway and entranceway was bursting with children's art. In one significant project, Principal Tracy worked with staff and parents to create a more vibrant playground. This involved painting the playground with an array of colors, investing in playground equipment, teaching all students playground games during physical education (so that everybody knew the same rules), staffing adults to both supervise and run games, teaching the older students to be playground helpers, and setting up a schedule so that all students participated in taking care of the playground. Tracy noted:

This program dramatically changed the nature of recess time—kids had more to do and were having more fun—and dramatically reduced playground conflicts. We reduced playground behavior referrals by 50% and cut suspensions from playground incidents by two thirds.

This focus on the playground not only reduced behavior issues but also created a sense of belonging for many students as they enjoyed their recess, had fun with one another, learned to handle and enjoy both cooperative and competitive games, and had one more place at school where they felt connected to other kids and to the school. One of Principal Tracy's goals was to infuse every event at school with excitement: "I really tried to make school fun." He talked about the "power of being visible, energetic, and knowing people's names. Staff and parents respond to leadership that exudes enthusiasm and passion about our students. Everybody likes it when you know them, and people blossom and are more committed when they feel important."

Since the definition of SJL used in this book centers on keeping marginalized students at the heart of the vision and practice, creating schools where these students felt connected, where they felt valued, and where they enjoyed being, positions these specific efforts as social justice advancements. Building strong relationships and creating a place where people were valued was a critical aspect across the schools and a fundamental part of the principals' approach to discipline.

Hart and Bredeson (1996) and Deal and Peterson (1999) describe the importance of the principal's creating a positive school climate. They argue that this climate is a necessary component to school improvement and increased academic learning of students. Scheurich (1998) found that building a child-centered culture of love, care, appreciation, and respect for both marginalized children and their families was central and imperative for diverse schools to create just environments that achieved high levels of student learning. The principals featured in this book also sought and achieved a similar goal by creating a warm and welcoming climate. An important complement to that warm school climate involved fostering classroom community building.

Foster Community Building in Each Classroom

The next strategy used to create a climate of belonging involved purposeful attention to building community in all classrooms. The principals felt that school should be a welcoming place where students, staff, and families wanted to be; however, a welcoming building, a respectful and gracious greeting, and a warm climate among adults was insufficient if that pleasant atmosphere did not extend into each classroom.

Principal Tracy's elementary school adopted a schoolwide community-building program called Tribes; each staff member received intensive training in how to teach using this program, which involved making time each day to develop community, first in "get to know you" ways, and then, as the year progressed, in deeper ways. Additionally, Tribes entailed adopting shared behavior norms and strategies for enhancing community throughout the day. The ideas, practices, and language permeated the entire school and the Tribes approach was used in every classroom as well as at staff meetings. Principal Tracy commented:

> It became clear that everyone was working to build community in similar ways. Certainly, for some, this was second nature, and for others, it was new and challenging, but you could feel the impact across the school and really in every classroom . . . walking into classrooms, seeing students valuing diversity in classroom conversations, and seeing how discipline was handled differently as a result.

While there are a number of community-building curricula and, admittedly, Tribes can be implemented both successfully and unsuccessfully, the main purpose and results of this effort were crucial in creating a climate of belonging for Tracy and other principals. As Principal Dale remarked:

> Paying purposeful attention to the community in the classroom is so integral to the success and learning of that classroom. Too often our middle and high school teachers do not attend to this, or only do "get to know you" activities during the first 2 days of school. Those same strategies can be incorporated into the teaching and learning each day. That way we are always consciously trying to enhance the connections and relationship between kids and between school and kids. This is a central part of making our inclusive changes and detracking work.

Principal Dale argued for and led his middle school to purposefully create community in each classroom as a priority. As a high school administrator, Principal Eli shared his strategy:

> It became night and day different. . . . Our teams of teachers focused attention to build relationships with all the kids they were responsible for. . . . As they worked to develop personal relationships, [the students] bought into better behavior. Some believe that focusing on relationships takes away from academics, but in our experience it enhanced it.

Principal Eli's school took a different approach to community: His school did not adopt a community-building program such as Tribes, but nonetheless there was emphasis on creating positive relationships between students as well as between students and their school. Principal Eli worked with his staff to be present in the hallway, get to know students in personal ways, and build and maintain a mentor relationship with three to four students whose behaviors or academic performance suggested trouble. Ferguson (1998), Kunc (1992), and Sapon-Shevin (2007) argue that community and relationship are essential to meaningful learning for each child as well as for working to close the achievement gap. This kind of community building was emphasized by the principals discussed here and became a key strategy in creating a climate of belonging. Further, they made concerted efforts to involve the diverse community in their schools.

Reach Out to Marginalized Families and the Community

The second strategy these principals used took the form of specifically and purposefully reaching out to marginalized families and community agencies. The principals discussed how involving the community and specifically reaching out to certain families made a difference in creating a more just school.

One way they did this was to make time to call, visit, and develop relationships with marginalized families. For example, in response to requests by families in her elementary school, Principal Meg and her staff started separate parent meetings for families of diverse ethnicities. Throughout the year they facilitated meetings for Hmong parents, Latino parents, and parents of African American students. According to Principal Meg, these forums "built community . . . strengthened connections between traditionally marginalized groups and our elementary school," and gave families both "information and a voice in their children's school." Some people disagreed with the idea of separate meetings for different ethnic groups and felt that this structure was "exclusive" and "segregating" and did not align with the inclusive school reforms; however, Minow (1990) has argued that the efforts of Principal Meg and her staff align with a broader understanding and spirit of inclusion, in that diverse families can attain more meaningful access to school and benefit from school involvement when the schools find ways to connect with and listen to more families. The result of the effort was that hundreds of families were involved at the school who previously had not been.

As with Principal Meg, the other six principals discussed the need for and their continuing efforts to build relationships with marginalized families. Principal Taylor commented that she "always set extra time aside to invite families" who were not traditionally vocal in her school and worked to "organize families to give input about heated issues who are often left out of the conversation by more privileged parents." Principal Eli discussed how he tried to be more visible in out-of-school settings:

> I need to be seen in the neighborhoods, out of school. Families who we
> had not connected with in the past have responded to positive, friendly,
> informal contact, whether it is by walking students home and chatting with
> families or attending neighborhood events to purely build relationships. I

have been able to meet more families and hear concerns that we had not heard before.

Principal Dale worked on the way families were greeted at the secondary level. He needed to be explicit with particular staff about how they addressed families and he needed to model respectful conversations:

> I worked with Mike [a teacher] who called home about a student's inappropriate behavior. Mike reported raising his voice and telling the kid's mom that "she needed to take responsibility" for the child's behavior. This made the mom very angry and later that day she stormed into Mike's office and then into my office to complain about how she was being treated. . . . This provided an opportunity to work with Mike. We talked about and even tried out some ways to handle these conversations in the future. I invited him to sit in on when I called a potentially volatile family about a behavior issue so he could see how I wanted him to be respectful. . . . The fact of the matter was, in many ways the school staff was turning certain families off to school by the disrespect we showed them in our conversations. But that was changeable.

The principals used outreach to connect their schools to traditionally marginalized families and neighborhoods. These leaders made time to involve families in new ways and developed mechanisms for listening and hearing from these families. In many ways, the leaders reframed how marginalized families were seen and respected at school.

The principals also sought to connect with the community agencies. At her high school, Principal Natalie "created partnerships with community agencies working on AOD [alcohol and other drug] issues. This provided a more seamless way to facilitate holistic services for our students." The principals knew the school could not meet all the needs of the children for whom they were responsible but saw a void of connection among services for children and families. They needed to make connections with community organizations and community providers, as there were services available in their cities.

Building a stronger base of support for both the schools and the families helped ease the disconnect between school and a marginalized community. For these principals, reaching out to the community and marginalized families was not rhetoric about community engagement or a distant understanding of "sub publics." It was about creating schools that include, value, and find ways to support families who traditionally have been marginalized by schools and society. Moving these families and their needs from the margin to the center fits with the definition of social justice used here, and by initiating projects and embodying attitudes that transformed their school and community climates, the principals made significant advances.

The literature on leadership for equity and justice provided a number of insights into reaching out to the community and marginalized families. Scheurich (1998) offered:

> These schools have created many different but creative ways to interweave the school and community, to create what Estes (1994) has called "the high performance learning community" (p. 28). But "this does not mean [that these schools are] re-socializing [for instance] African-American parents to White middle-class ways" (Hollins & Spencer, 1990, p. 93); instead, these schools experience themselves as being in union with the community—the community's needs and dreams are their needs and dreams, and vice versa. (p. 466)

Goldfarb and Grinberg (2002) concluded that community ownership and connection are essential components to a successful organization striving for social justice. The principals in this book carried out the mission that Scheurich as well as Goldfarb and Grinberg put forth.

Incorporate Social Responsibility into the School Curriculum

The next strategy that the principals discussed using to overcome the disconnect between a marginalized community and school took the form of incorporating social responsibility into the curriculum. The principals relayed that their schools emphasized involvement in the community to improve student learning. Principal Eli described designing the high school mission and "lessons that really connect with the community, to see how what they've learned in the classroom can impact the community":

> Kids as a part of their curriculum are doing various projects in which they're studying the community and what it doesn't have in order to come up with either businesses or nonprofits or collaborative ventures that fill the gaps . . . to understand what works or doesn't work so that they can have a positive impact on their neighborhood. . . . They'll do collective action, not just be an individual.

Eli stated that both students and faculty were embracing and discussing ideas of collective action during informal conversations, official school meetings, and courses (for instance, student involvement in studying and engaging in community organizing, class lessons about social movements or grassroots organizing).

Principal Natalie discussed the idea of "restorative justice" as a major concept instituted in her high school. Students were taught to mediate and deal with violations to the school's code of conduct, and "every day was a new day." With the new day came an expectation and "a chance to repair any damage that happened." Principal Natalie also described courses designed to connect students to communities not only in order to create meaningful learning but also to reinforce a connection to something larger than oneself:

> We tried to offer more of these types of classes. . . . There is a community in Mississippi, settled by African American individuals before the Civil War, and then they kept the community until now, which was holy hell during that time of extreme violence. . . . Our kids have gone down there and they have helped document their history because a lot of their elders are passing away and they want a documentation of their history.

In both these examples, principals sought to establish norms in their schools to include teaching social responsibility. While incorporating service and social responsibility in the curriculum started as additions to the yearly schedule, both service and social responsibility were eventually integrated into a curriculum plan.

A critical component to creating socially just classrooms and schools is teaching students the skills and responsibilities to create their own social change (Ayers, Hunt, & Quinn, 1998; Freire, 1990; Purpel, 1989). By promoting social responsibility, the principals moved beyond equal access for marginalized students to establish an emancipatory and action-oriented pedagogy for their schools. This resonates with what Ayers et al., Freire, and Purpel called for in creating socially just classrooms, and their actions made significant and meaningful connections to the community. The social action the principals advanced was also seen in the literature on leadership in Brown's (2004) call for "activist action plans" to be incorporated into administrator training as a means of instilling a sense of agency and social responsibility in future principals. However, instilling the skills to take social action was neither a part of traditional administrator preparation nor central to the literature on SJL.

Use a Proactive and Process Approach to Discipline

As was stated in the beginning of this chapter, creating a climate of belonging was an entirely different way to approach discipline. The final strategy the principals used involved a proactive and process approach to discipline. The seven principals felt that the four other strategies presented in this chapter were integral parts of their approach to discipline. Principal Natalie explained this for her high school:

Building relationships with students, creating community in classrooms and across the school, instilling a sense of responsibility to [the] immediate community, along with developing deeper connections to families are essential. What many people seem to forget is that these are really the building blocks of changing student behavior and an effective approach to discipline.

She is recognizing that the other strategies that she and the other six principals used were intimately connected to her way of thinking about student behavior and discipline.

Principal Eli continued to elaborate on this proactive approach to high school discipline:

We have a metal detector—a remnant from the mega high school that previously inhabited this space. And we have not ripped it down, but it is not the cornerstone of our discipline or safety plan. I suppose for some it makes them feel safer and for some it makes them feel less safe. But at this school now, safety comes from students having relationship with adults and students feeling connected to their school and involved in their community. Compared to the old way—expecting bad behavior, catching students, and punishing—now we have a much lower percentage of students getting in trouble and being sent home.

Principal Eli explained that the traditional security measures, such as metal detectors, while still a part of his school, are being figuratively replaced by a climate of belonging. This shift in approach toward discipline has actually decreased the percentage of students involved in negative behavior and, as a result, decreased the severe consequences placed upon marginalized students.

Principal Dale discussed zero-tolerance policies and moving away from relying on police for school discipline:

My district has a zero-tolerance policy and I do have to follow it. But that mainly only applies to weapons and drugs. The vast majority of discipline issues are for things that are not black and white in nature. They are much more gray, like "inappropriate behavior" or language or attitude or even pushing and shoving. These offenses cannot be punished away. We need to sit down, discuss, and educate kids. We need to listen to what they are telling us, and then have them make amends for their behavior. Calling the police on a 13-year-old who is disrespectful does not change the behavior and only sentences that child to be part of the criminal system perhaps forever.

Principal Dale felt a lot of resistance from some staff and parents for this approach to discipline—for not suspending more students and not calling the police more often. He maintained that processing with students and having them come to terms with their misbehavior was more powerful. As mentioned earlier, during his tenure his school experienced a significant reduction in behavior referrals and suspensions. It is important to note that the hard data collected about discipline referrals before Principal Dale's time did not include students with special education labels. After inclusive restructuring, students with special education needs were included in the discipline system. Thus, even while including students with the most significant behavior issues, Principal Dale saw large reductions in negative student behavior.

All seven principals followed a similar philosophical approach to student discipline. Yet none had a prescribed way to deal with children (no point systems, no 1, 2, 3 magic). They and their support staff talked with students, processed with groups of students involved in conflicts, found ways for students to resolve situations when they had hurt or offended people, and always involved families in these discussions. For these leaders, discipline was a process and ultimately a learning experience for those involved. Some of the principals, but not all, were criticized by some staff for being too soft on students and having lax discipline standards. While there are always varying perspectives on this, the leaders expected high levels of student behavior and followed the district code of conduct. Principal Scott said,

> I took a stand with the staff and students: There will be no racial or gay name-calling. Absolutely no using *nigger* or *faggot*. It took a commitment, but those words disappeared from our school.

Principal Scott took seriously that hate language was unacceptable, and his answer was not to simply exclude or suspend students. Instead, he came back again and again to educating students about why those words were not allowed and forced students to make amends to those whom they had offended. Principal Tracy followed a similar approach. For example, if his elementary students were involved in vandalism, they were then responsible for helping to repair the damage. Then, when the school moved to the new playground program (discussed earlier in this chapter), all students were responsible for weekly maintenance and upkeep of the playground and school area. This combination of expecting students to take care of and be responsible for their school and their classmates resonated throughout Principal Tracy's approach.

Discipline issues plague many schools, manifested as chaotic environments or rigid, almost militaristic ones that embody the belief that the students in those places cannot handle freedom or latitude or places where yelling and intimidation are the main forms of control for marginalized students. Part of getting a hold of the discipline problem comes from thinking about it differently. The principals discussed here did just that. Their proactive, process-oriented, holistic view of discipline and student behavior not only reduced suspensions and behavior referrals at their school but also was part of a larger vision of developing a climate of belonging.

CONCLUSION

In connection with their proactive approach to discipline, the principals worked to create more just schools by fostering a warm and welcoming climate, reaching out and valuing the community and marginalized families, and infusing social responsibility into the curriculum. They also focused on building a school climate and classroom community where students developed connections with each other, a deeper understanding and respect for diversity, and a sense that each of them was an important member of the school. These leaders appeared to move beyond lip service about climate and diversity to building a school culture that embraced diversity and connected in meaningful ways with the community. They shared ways they worked to bridge the school-community divide and, in doing so, demonstrated that school administration has the responsibility to bridge that divide and is capable of doing so. By taking a stance that their schools needed to honor and respect all families (and in particular marginalized families), they moved beyond a condescending or infantilizing view of disconnected families and helped their staff members move philosophically in this direction as well. These strategies were used to transform schools into welcoming places where marginalized families were valued and connected to the education of their children.

While many educators and scholars discuss the importance of developing ways for schools to work with families, these practicing leaders embody a different understanding of school-family and school-community relationships. As was the case with how they moved beyond instructional leadership with their social justice stance, these principals again moved beyond typical home-school relations. They did not separate the climate at school from the ways in which families, students, and staff felt connected and developed relationships. Moreover, they made a purposeful connection between climate and school discipline. The seven principals purposefully developed a climate in which all staff members were deemed important, where students learned to respect each other, and where the diversity of families was valued, not marginalized. Clearly, this is not a fixed target or an accomplishment to be checked off. Understanding creating a climate of belonging in the way these leaders did positions SJL as a dynamic effort without a fixed goal to be completed. This notion of SJL sees the role of school leaders as continually pushing and finding ways to foster community and belonging for all and, in particular, for those who are traditionally marginalized.

Many school leaders mourn the lack of involvement of families in schools, particularly from low-income families and families of color. Many leaders know the importance of home-school relations, yet this is often translated into calling homes about discipline issues, working with the official (and often small) parent organization, or sending information home via a school newsletter. While the principals here engaged in all those behaviors, they also purposefully found ways to get more families involved in school beyond these traditional vehicles. SJL recognizes that schools must be welcoming places for families from the moment they enter the school and in every interaction thereafter. The principals acted on that conviction by working not only to connect to families but also to ensure that children felt that school was a community in which to learn, feel important, and respect others. The principals extended their understanding of belonging by reaching out and engaging community members and organizations outside the walls of the school. Central to their work was an ongoing effort to change the injustice of an unwelcoming school climate that perpetuated the alienation of disconnected families, community, and students.

It is evident that in many schools, discipline issues consume school leaders. In positioning discipline from this alternate paradigm—whereby student behavior is necessarily connected to issues of belonging—these seven leaders provided an authentic view into a proactive, process-oriented, holistic approach. Developing a climate of belonging, as well as working to increase inclusion, access, and opportunities in an improved and improving core teaching and curriculum created a more equitable and just school experience. In these schools more and more students were intimately involved in serious and nurturing general education classrooms that fostered community, within an environment in which they, their teachers, and their families felt connected to each other and to the school. As Principal Dale concludes,

> Our school will fail unless we can build an authentic community among our students, families, and teachers. This is not rocket science, but it will not happen by itself. We will never be able to include all students meaningfully until we do so, nor will we be able to deeply engage all students in learning until we create and maintain that community. This is not only possible, but it is imperative.

Closing the Achievement Gap: Toward a Theory of Socially Just School Reform

I long to accomplish a great and noble task, but it is my chief duty to accomplish small tasks as if they were great and noble.

—Helen Keller

I N MANY regards, raising student achievement (in particular the achievement of marginalized students) is often seen as a great and insurmountable task. This task is a primary calling of SJL, but as described here, the principals combined, in the words of Helen Keller, numerous "small tasks as if they were great and noble" that they felt led to their ability to raise student learning and make significant strides to close the achievement gap at their schools.

One of the greatest injustices these principals felt compelled to change was low levels of student learning and the achievement gap between marginalized students and their peers that is so prevalent in educational discussion of the 21st century. This chapter illustrates how the seven principals improved the achievement of all students through their ability to lead with another key to SJL:

Key 6. Raise student achievement.

All seven principals believed that raising student achievement, in particular the achievement of traditionally marginalized students, was a central focus in making their schools more just. Six of the seven described improvements in academic achievement during their tenure at their schools. The seventh principal, in the first year at his school, emphasized the areas needed for improvement, but in reality, there had not been much time to see any significant change in achievement. All the achievement data the principals discussed was verified with their state educational agencies; however, in keeping with the spirit of allowing these leaders to narrate their experience, I primarily use their voice to explain the achievement gains.

While disparate and low achievement was the greatest injustice the seven principals felt they worked to reverse, there is no list of strategies governing their accomplishments of this goal. Instead, they saw their commitment to the achievement of marginalized students, as one principal put it, as "permeating everything I did, every decision I made, every conversation I had, and every part of my leadership." To reflect this, the present chapter will follow a slightly different structure from the other three that also focused on correcting injustices. First, like the previous three, this chapter uses the principals' voices to articulate the connection they saw between social justice and raising student achievement. Next, it provides five examples of the kinds of raises in student achievement these principals realized during their tenure. Finally, it positions all the strategies they evoked from challenging the first three injustices (Chapters 3, 4, and 5) as the foundation for the improvements in achievement. This foundation provides an emerging theory of social justice school reform and improvement.

THE CONNECTION BETWEEN RAISING STUDENT ACHIEVEMENT AND SOCIAL JUSTICE

In the current era of standards and accountability, raising student achievement is on the minds of most, if not all, school leaders—not only leaders committed to equity and social justice. However, the principals featured in this book articulate the connection they saw between social justice and raising student achievement.

While all the principals were critical of standardized testing measures, they were adamant that the marginalized students at their schools could and would be successful. All shared a similar perspective that the push for testing would ultimately harm schools and marginalized students. They saw high-stakes testing as creating a very narrow definition of student achievement and school success. They felt this definition was being and would continue to be used to narrow opportunities, with increasing attention being paid only to remedial reading and mathematics for marginalized students. They knew that testing of this kind historically has privileged some students and kept others on the margins. Yet these leaders all had what they defined as a "moral obligation" to ensure that their marginalized students were successful on the tests. They sought to achieve this through authentic and engaging teaching and learning, not test prep or skill-and-drill. This thinking was paradoxical in how it positioned testing accountability as what one principal called "an evil" but also "as a moral duty to keep track of students."

Principal Tracy explained his thoughts regarding raising student achievement and social justice:

> We have an obligation to understand and monitor the achievement of all students. Historically, we have only kept track of some students. While I

do not agree with or like the state high-stakes testing, we can use it as another vehicle to keep track of data about our most vulnerable students. This is really important, as it is not enough to be nice and to tolerate these students, it is not enough to talk about inclusion, we have an obligation to make sure our students are academically strong, particularly the most vulnerable ones. We have to make sure they are performing at high levels.

This principal describes a position that equates social justice with understanding how students are achieving and, more important, ensures that students who have traditionally struggled or failed are successful at school. As Principal Scott stated,

We cannot talk about [social justice] without being ultimately concerned about student achievement. We know what a potentially grim future that is out there for students who leave us without being able to read or without strong math-thinking ability. I do not take this lightly.

In short, the principals argued that we have not achieved much in the way of justice and equity if we do not or cannot raise these horribly disparate levels of student achievement. Across their schools, when they arrived, the seven principals found 24% of African American students on track to graduate high school, 13% of students with disabilities reading at elementary grade level, and no students learning English passing the state reading exams. Without all students and particularly students from marginalized groups becoming increasingly proficient on state exams, I concur with these leaders, we are perpetuating injustice. Thus, raising student achievement is a central component of SJL.

RAISING STUDENT ACHIEVEMENT

Certainly in an era of standards and accountability, raising student achievement is an expectation of all schools. The principals articulated an important connection between social justice and achievement. While they were concerned about state tests and saw it as essential that particularly marginalized students are successful and are proficient at their grade level, they also included broader school data to understand student achievement. Given the messy and continuing nature of their work and the small number of principals used here to illustrate SJL, this is in no way proof that any one of the strategies they used resulted in or will result in increased achievement. This section describes the kinds of improvements they experienced, positioned alongside the work, struggle, and vision they maintained. Five examples follow of the kinds of increases in student achievement these leaders saw.

Principal Tracy's Elementary School

Principal Tracy's school saw much growth in student achievement in 3 years' time. Performance of all students as well as disaggregated data from particular groups of students show tremendous growth on state reading exams (Table 6.1) as well as locally developed reading assessments and sustained achievement gains in language arts on the state accountability test (Figure 6.1). It is important to note that over the course of data presented from Principal Tracy's school, prior to Principal Tracy's arrival 70% of the student body were given achievement tests and 3 years later 98% were. Students who had been typically excluded were thought to be incapable of achieving at grade level. Thus the data presented reflect that increase in the number of students who previously had been thought to not be able to "pass" the tests.

Principal Eli's High School

Principal Eli discussed the rapid improvements he saw in high school student achievement and how those improvements were central to his mission. On state tests, his students improved from 15% of the students achieving at grade-level norms to 45% over a 3-year period; moreover, the disaggregated data show that low-income students and students of color achieved exactly the same gains. He also saw vast improvements in graduation rates, from 25% of the ninth-grade cohort

Table 6.1. Student achievement on statewide reading test.

	Percent of students scoring at or above grade level the year before Principal Tracy arrived	Percent of students scoring at or above grade level 3 years later
All students	50	86
African American students	33	78
Asian students	47	100
Hispanic students	18	100
Special education students	13	60
ELL students	17	100
Students in poverty	40	78

Notes: Adapted from Theoharis, 2007. Student categories are based on state classifications. Grade level is determined by the state's performance levels for students.

Figure 6.1. Students with disabilities scoring at or above grade level on statewide fourth-grade exam.

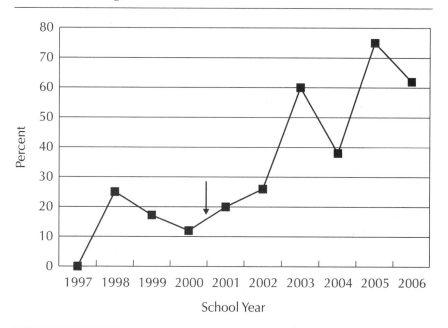

Note: Arrow indicates when Principal Tracy began as principal at this school.

graduating in 4 years to 85% on track to graduate in 4 years. Principal Eli revealed a mix of pride and dissatisfaction in discussing these data, because while it was "significant improvement, many students still seriously struggled."

Principal Dale's Middle School

Principal Dale also realized achievement gains as part of his work in advancing social justice. For the past 3 years, the state Department of Education had named his middle school a "Promise School of Recognition." Principal Dale reported that the school was given this award because it was in the top quartile of the state in the percentage of students who receive free or reduced-price lunch and demonstrated above-average student academic performance in reading and mathematics for all students and student groups.

Principal Dale explained that over the past 5 years under his leadership, reading and math achievement rose from "around 65% of students achieving proficient or advanced to 84%." Over that time, science and social studies achievement remained fairly steady. When he started as principal at his school, only "78% of the students were being tested and now 98% are. More students are taking the tests, which would make you think that our percentages of students achieving proficient or advanced would decrease. But the numbers of students doing well has grown across all subjects." When the data are disaggregated by race, income, and ability, students of color, students from low-income families and students with disabilities show the most gains.

Principal Meg's Elementary School

Principal Meg also saw achievement gains for her elementary students. She explained that White, middle-income students traditionally scored well on most local and state assessments because of the school's location in a large upper-middle class, university community. She said that there was significant room for improvement for her students of color and students learning English. When Principal Meg started at her school, none of the students learning English took the third-grade state mandated reading test, because it was assumed that they would not pass. After restructuring and every student being tested on district assessments, and nearly every student on state tests, Principal Meg reported:

> We had over a 90% pass rate for our Latino students on the third-grade reading test, with only one student not taking the test. This was much higher percentages than the district and higher than the state for that particular group of kids. We had always scored high for our White, university kids, but now our students of color and students learning English are excelling too.

Principal Meg mentioned that her "African American students are scoring higher than district peers," meaning that they consistently outperformed district norms and averages in the primary grades on district assessments. She divulged her need to make even more improvements for her African American, Latino, and Hmong students: "We're doing better, we're more accountable, we have better data, but we need to do more for some of our Black and Brown kids."

Principal Natalie's High School

Principal Natalie provides an example of how these leaders also used different types of student achievement data other than state-mandated tests to understand and explain raises in student achievement. No data were kept on measures of achievement before she started at her high school. All the data reported reflects data she has kept, starting in her first year. Previously about 15% of the students failed their classes at school, but this had improved to only 7% failing. While the "critics could claim we have lowered our standards, the opposite is actually true. We are expecting much more academically from our kids."

Principal Natalie explained that now 79% of her students went on to college, whereas only 68% had when she arrived. The American College Test (ACT) composite score for her students remained steady at 23. Seen in conjunction with a rise in students attending postsecondary institutions, a rise in students taking the ACT, a dramatic increase in students with disabilities attending her school from 3% to 23%, and a rise from 11% students of color at this school to 34%, "this maintenance of the ACT composite score signifies that more marginalized students are not only taking the ACT, but are achieving more success."

In comparing these advances with what is stated in the literature on leading for social justice, this success with raising student achievement paralleled what Riester et al. (2002) and Scheurich (1998) found. Both Scheurich and Riester et al. examined schools where marginalized students performed at high academic levels. Scheurich stated that students at these schools achieved at levels "placing them in direct academic competition with what are considered the better Anglo-dominated schools" (p. 452). This was also true of the principals' schools. While not every school or particular demographic group in each school discussed here outperformed students in affluent and privileged schools, the gains in student achievement were notable. Some students from marginalized backgrounds in the principals' schools outperformed or matched their more privileged peers and the achievement trajectory for others remains promising. This reality supports what the literature has shown is possible for schools serving students from marginalized groups.

Raising student achievement is a goal for many school administrators, and achieving this goal per se is not in and of itself social justice work. Among the schools discussed here, dramatic academic gains were seen for marginalized students. Whereas many high-performing schools or high-performing districts struggle with disparate achievement for marginalized students, the gains at the schools where the principals featured here and their ability to raise student achievement levels clearly distinguish this phenomenon from traditional school improvement and centers the advancement as social justice work.

TOWARD A THEORY OF SOCIALLY JUST SCHOOL REFORM

Understanding the ways in which the principals changed the other three injustices involved examining the strategies they used. Here, however, there were no explicit strategies. Contrary to how most people talk about advancing student achievement, the principals moved the conversation away from a linear and clearly delineated process—to one that requires doing many, many things.

Currently, school improvement has been reduced to a discussion of how schools can raise test scores and, more specifically, raise the test scores of enough students right below the cusp of passing so that annual yearly progress can be demonstrated. These efforts typically follow similar paths involving identifying and sorting students based on performance on state assessments. Teams of school staff members then mine the state assessment data for gaps, looking for questions or areas where significant numbers of students answered incorrectly. And if things go well, the teachers then try to address both the content gaps and the kinds of thinking required on the test. Much money, energy, and time are used to tackle examining this data and creating plans. Students, typically those below the passing cusp, are then provided (subjected to) various assortments of remedial programs and instruction to target their individual needs at their individual levels. Such school improvement efforts have created increasing numbers of separate programs (the Academic Intervention Services [AIS], remedial reading, and so on), trying to provide a booster shot to struggling students in order to raise achievement. These separate programs are increasingly tracking or grouping students by achievement and then giving struggling students a narrower curriculum, using a drill-and-practice approach for greater amounts of time during the school day.

This is often combined with test preparation—meaning taking time to teach students test-taking skills. Along with these steps, schools often try to use the formats used on the test in other aspects of the curriculum so students are familiar with the test formats. These demands to improve scores has also created pressure to reduce the time for subjects and activities not on the high-stakes test (music, science, recess). Schmoker (2006) reported that this traditional response to school improvement has made no real difference in substantially improving schools. And there is a growing body of research to show that the curriculum has become narrower and that marginalized students have been given less access to rich experiences and more access to drill and practice.

In contrast to this approach, the leaders looked much more holistically at school improvement. To better understand how they raised student achievement, I propose an emerging theory of social justice school reform/improvement. This theory requires a three-legged approach (see Figure 6.2). The precarious nature of a three-legged stool illustrates the complexity and uncertainty of school reform and, in particular, the precarious nature of raising students' achievement for marginalized students. However, when taken together, these three legs are a powerful means to understanding and creating meaningful, equitable, and just school reform.

The leaders believed that the sum of their efforts to increase inclusion, access, and opportunity; to improve the core learning context; and to create a climate of belonging became the combined ways they raised student achievement. In contrast to narrowing the curriculum and providing remediation, they took a much broader perspective on school reform. This emerging theory illustrates three legs that support raising student achievement. The first leg is increasing access to the core learning—described by the principals in Chapter 3. The second leg is

Figure 6.2. Three-legged approach to social justice school reform.

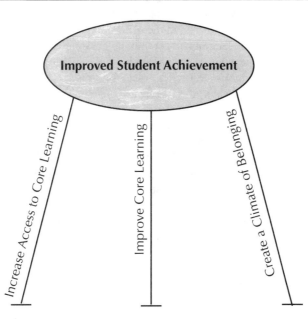

improving the core learning context, both the teaching and curriculum—detailed in Chapter 4. The third leg is creating a climate of belonging—discussed in Chapter 5. When taken together, as was the case for the principals, these three legs created a stool by which student achievement was boosted.

Principal Dale's middle school provides an example of these three legs coming together to boost student achievement. Previously, students were spending increasing amounts of time in achievement-level-based groups for literacy and were tracked for math, and student with disabilities were educated separately. Principal Dale led a restructuring so that all students were grouped heterogeneously across grade level and teams of specialists and content area teachers team-taught and co-planned the daily lessons. This gave all students access to the core learning context (first leg of the stool).

That core learning context, however, was not static. Principal Dale and his staff worked collaboratively to improve that context through adopting and learning about constructivist math, engaging in ongoing professional learning and discussions of race, and offering significant opportunities for specialists and general educators to come together to learn to collaborate. Principal Dale facilitated these key aspects of improving the core learning context as well as hired new staff and supervised all staff to meet these expectations (second leg of the stool).

This increasing access and improving the core learning context took place during the creation of the climate of belonging. Principal Dale led a campaign to make the school more welcoming by positively changing how staff greeted students and visitors in the hallways, in the office, and in classrooms. The teachers took part in professional learning on community building within their classrooms. The vast majority of teachers purposefully built community throughout the year in their classes. Principal Dale used a process-oriented discipline approach and focused on discussing issues with students and engaging them in making amends. Principal Dale and the staff built bridges to local community agencies and specific families (third leg of the stool). Over a 5-year period of these reforms, student achievement for all groups rose substantially.

This three-legged approach suggests that efforts to tackle only one avenue of school reform may indeed be insufficient for increasing the achievement of marginalized students. A common strategy is adopting new curriculum and taking a strong focus on professional development (as in a new reading series and staff training around the philosophy and skills needed to deliver it). This alone is insufficient if structures continue to isolate and separate students and a climate that values and includes all is not present. In this case, while it is possible that some students are receiving a better education, many marginalized students will not have access to the improved teaching and curriculum and will endure the daily unwelcoming climate. That lack of access and poor climate can perpetuate low student achievement. Likewise, just including students who have been traditionally removed from general education, which, in the words of the principals is a moral and social justice accomplishment in itself, might not realize improved achievement if these students now have access to inadequate teaching and curriculum. Also, focusing on a warm climate and developing meaningful relationship with families and community alone will not raise achievement if the structures and core learning context are left unaffected. In understanding the SJL of these seven principals, this emerging theory of socially just school reform presents a way to approach tackling the struggles schools face in fully educating all students.

CHAPTER 7

"At Every Turn": The Barriers Faced by Social Justice Principals

"EVERY DAY, *at every turn*, from every direction, I run up against barriers to this equity work," commented Principal Meg when asked about the resistance she faced in trying to enact a social justice agenda. While these principals helped to transform their schools into more just environments for students and staff, they encountered tremendous barriers. The principals reported that their work felt like a constant uphill struggle. This chapter moves outside the framework illustrated in Chapter 1.

The purpose of this chapter is to build an understanding about the barriers that principals face while leading for social justice. In creating equitable and excellent schools, it is imperative to understand the historical, political, and educational barriers that exist when leaders seek to create more socially just schools.

I recognize that some scholars and school leaders use the term *barriers* and others use *pressures* or *tensions* or *resistance* against achieving equity. For the purpose of this chapter, I will use the term *barriers* to mean all the resistance, countervailing pressures, tensions, and realities that detract from leading to create more equitable and just schools.

In understanding SJL, I purposefully selected not only principals committed to social justice, but also those who had reached success in moving their schools in that direction as described in Chapters 3–6. I position the formidable barriers the principals faced within the progress they achieved moving toward more equitable and just schools purposefully for two reasons. First, this allows for a serious understanding of the barriers, and second, while these barriers were indeed significant it is important to recognize that creating more just and equitable schools is possible.

These principals described barriers from different aspects of their organizations: the school site, the district, and the institutional level. This discussion begins with the pressures that were most intimate to the daily work of these leaders, the barriers from within their school sites. It then moves to the pressures from the district, then to the institutional level. This chapter concludes with the leaders' descriptions of the personal and professional consequences that occurred as a result of the resistance they faced, from diverse avenues within the school/community and from the district and beyond. Figure 7.1 provides an organized view of this resistance.

BARRIERS WITHIN THE SCHOOL SITE

"It is an almost impossible job," stated one of the principals while discussing barriers to following her drive to enact social justice. The resistance to advancing social justice within the local school/community came through four avenues: the vast scope of the principalship, the momentum of the status quo, obstructive staff beliefs and behaviors, and insular/privileged parental attitudes.

The Vast Scope of the Principalship

The principals experienced how the vast scope of their position created significant pressure against doing equity and justice work. Principal Dale believed that the tasks of the principal, "the reports, the paperwork, the sheer number of people

Figure 7.1. The resistance principals face.

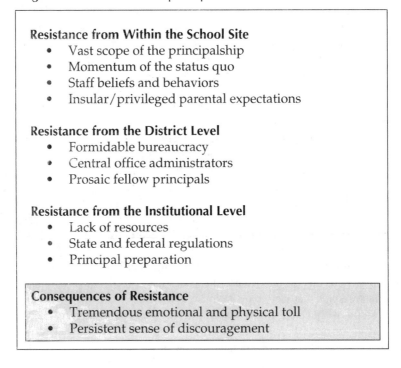

Resistance from Within the School Site
- Vast scope of the principalship
- Momentum of the status quo
- Staff beliefs and behaviors
- Insular/privileged parental expectations

Resistance from the District Level
- Formidable bureaucracy
- Central office administrators
- Prosaic fellow principals

Resistance from the Institutional Level
- Lack of resources
- State and federal regulations
- Principal preparation

Consequences of Resistance
- Tremendous emotional and physical toll
- Persistent sense of discouragement

to deal with," all put a strain on one's ability to do the important work of making the school more equitable. He relayed that this meant feeling as though one had time for only the most "marginal" staff or the most immediate issues. He felt that these people or issues took up so much of his time that the big picture and proactive work to change "inequitable norms" always took a backseat. Principal Scott had a similar feeling about the realities of the principal position:

> Working with teachers on culturally relevant teaching and behavior management is something I should be doing more. I should make more time for that. But how much time can I make when I already have less time than I need. . . . The paperwork, the truancy reports, the expulsion reports, lunchroom duty . . . the stuff to keep the school running, the list goes on and on. All that other stuff takes 10 to 12 hours a day.

The principals spoke of the pressure they felt was heaped on them because of the nature of the principalship. They agreed that the amount and variety of required tasks impeded their ability to purposefully work on their social justice agenda. While it is documented that all principals face an ever growing amount of responsibility, the leaders I studied who brought to their schools an equity and social justice agenda argued not that they had more demands but that the typical demands affected them in different ways. This resulted in internal stress for the leaders. They expressed never feeling able to "do enough" to change the realities for marginalized students because of being pulled in so many directions. In addition to the "10 to 12 hours" of tasks that all principals face, these leaders experienced additional pressure because of their awareness of the justice and equity issues inherent in each responsibility.

Principal Natalie felt the pressure she put upon herself as a result of the enormity of the job and not being able to serve the students in the manner she felt they deserved:

> There is so much that has to be done, and I can't sleep at night, I can't. A lot of times I can't even go home until it's done, which means I work 12, 14, 16 hours some days because I got to feel like I am making some progress to change things for the kids we failed for too long. . . . I can't go home until . . . I have researched whatever this student needs for tomorrow; I've talked to this person or that parent or this probation officer. . . . I always want to fix everything. I feel that I can fix everything, but there is so much else too, so I put this enormous stress on myself; I have to take care of it.

Principal Tracy also discussed the expectation of the role manifested in pressure/resistance he placed upon himself:

I vividly remember this struggle in thinking about a boy named Jerome, an African American student. I would see him sitting in the hallway because he was in trouble again. He was in kindergarten, and I saw him becoming really disenfranchised from school and it was his first year there. I felt, I just cannot change the system, teacher's attitudes, and skills, and people's worldview fast enough to keep Jerome safe from what we were doing to him. I could see all these things that were wrong and I needed to do something about them because I was the principal. That killed me, because I could see what I could do to change things, but I could not achieve those results fast enough. That made me think I needed to quit. I would be internally sad for days, for months.

These principals divulged deeply personal feelings about their need to make a substantial difference for their most marginalized and vulnerable students. They also conveyed a sense of constantly questioning their adequacy, skills, and abilities to actually do the job they believed needed to be done.

Manasse (1985) reported that principals have as many as 400 interactions and as many as 150 separate events a day. Adding this to the current placement of greater and greater demands on the principalship with fewer resources (Kinney, 2003; Langer & Boris-Schacter, 2003; Marshall, 2004; Shields et al., 2002; Strachan, 1997) speaks to the overwhelming size and scope of the position. The countervailing pressure that the position itself puts on enacting social justice created the situation that Scheurich and Skrla (2003) described as nearly impossible conditions.

In terms of the immense personal expectations and the pressures and barriers produced by enacting social justice, Rapp (2002) argued that within the current system, administrators are left to believe that if they just did everything right, "there would be more peace, higher wages, less hatred, more leisure time, greater voter turnout, less crime (including corporate), fewer terrorists attacks, and more social justice" (p. 229). He asserts that this is simply not true and the social and political realities of accountability and standards create this erroneous belief. Certainly the personal pressure that the principals reported are echoed in the hegemonic system that Rapp discussed. In addition to both the intrinsic and extrinsic resistance from the principalship, the momentum of the status quo created resistance that these principals felt was pushing against their equity and justice work.

Momentum of the Status Quo

The momentum of the status quo was the second barrier from within the school site. One principal stated that "years of maintaining particular, inequitable school norms and structures generated a considerable amount of momentum." Leaders seeking to change these norms and structures faced formidable pressure against their change efforts. Principal Taylor came to her elementary school and found a group in the community who grew accustomed to having their "demands, wishes, and whims" catered to by the principal. She found an experienced staff who for years had done "their own thing—some of it was good for kids and some of it not," and that the staff had "grown comfortable with weak and complacent leadership." Principal Taylor described this combination as creating considerable momentum against her social justice agenda. Both the community group and the teachers were used to doing "their own thing" in different ways, but Principal Taylor found that the combination of these factors had led to particular inequities in programming and outcomes for students of color and low-income students. It is important to understand that Principal Taylor became an outspoken advocate for her teachers, but the momentum she found when she started at her school worked against centering decisions on marginalized students.

Principal Tracy felt a communal lack of urgency for examining practices and programs:

> Much of the staff felt like they had done things really well for a long time, and certainly that was true, but only in part. I felt the attitude was, "We're a great school, we've done it this way for a long time and we do things really well. The kids are successful." In examining the realities of our school, the kids who were successful were always the same White middle-class kids. . . . I heard from district administrators and the superintendent . . . they had 15 years of "complacent" leadership. To me this felt like there had been no leadership looking at why the same kids were always getting the short end of the stick.

Principal Meg found structural issues of the status quo that made equity in schools more difficult:

> One example of this is the bus routes getting too long for kids of color for summer school. . . . The way it worked was that many of our ELL students, our Brown students, rode buses for up to 45 minutes each way. They had to travel across town, to attend a summer school program. Certainly no one was making any of the White affluent kids ride across town for 45 minutes. Are the Brown kids supposed to be thankful just to have the opportunity? And that makes it OK to ship them all over? I mean, come on!

She found these kinds of structures in place in her elementary school and across her district. In the case of bus schedules, changing them has a domino effect on people, schools, and programs across the school district. This created an "incredible momentum" against looking at more equitable busing or programming structures that might have better served the ELL students whom Meg felt were being "wronged."

The principals described feeling trapped, stuck, and frustrated while they struggled against the momentum that had built up over many years. Changing the structures that resisted more equitable schools and shifting school norms proved to be an enormous task.

The inequity the principals found in the status quo is echoed and illuminated by other scholars. Shields (2004) noted that despite well-intentioned reform and restructuring efforts, the status quo maintained inequitable levels of performance, access, and achievement. She reported that changing the status quo required complex thinking and deep understanding of diverse issues where inequities created by the status quo would have to be resolved, thus making socially just change more difficult. Oakes et al. (2000) found that stakeholders benefiting from the status quo increased the difficulty of making justice-oriented changes that threatened historic patterns and conditions. These scholars' findings verify the magnitude of the tasks the principals faced in attempting to change inequitable aspects of the status quo. Along with the momentum of the status quo, the principals felt persistent resistance from obstructive staff attitudes and beliefs.

Obstructive Staff Beliefs and Behaviors

The third location of resistance from within the school/community was obstructive staff beliefs and behaviors. The attitudes, beliefs, and actions of certain individuals and groups of staff resulted in pressure to not do this work. For this section I will not use the pseudonyms, so to further protect the principals from being identified and any repercussions this might cause.

One principal noted that many talented teachers worked at the school, but a common attitude embodied a belief that "because I am working with a needy and challenging population I should be able to do whatever I want. The students can take it or leave it." This principal stated, "The staff felt, they have wonderful gifts to give kids, and if the kids don't want it the way the staff give it, that's too bad for the kids."

A second principal found a number of staff members' lack of interest in reflecting on their practices or beliefs about children to be both troubling and a source of resistance. This principal felt that these attitudes took a combination of overt and subtle forms:

> I heard from teacher after teacher that particular students—who inevitably were students of color, low-income students, or students with disabilities— needed to be removed from the classroom, punished, sent home, or excluded from academic and social time. I did not believe these teachers hated these children or were overtly classist or racist or ableist about them.

This principal felt that the teachers were often looking for someone else to help this child succeed. In that wanting someone else to help that child, he felt that the teachers wanted to give up that responsibility themselves:

> One instance involved a second-grade teacher who had sent out the same African American boy from her classroom for 9 days in a row. She was clear that she wanted that child "out." We discussed that we all knew he was in the process of being assessed for special education and in all likelihood he would receive special education support, but that he would need support in her classroom, not in isolation by himself. I could not help feeling that she was setting this child up to fail and as a result be labeled as "disabled" and it was at least in part due to how he was being treated by her. From my perspective, this teacher did not want to engage with this child. I felt, heard, and saw how she demanded that if this second-grade boy could not do what everyone else was doing in the moment they were doing it, then she did not want him. I confronted this over and over and I tried to improve the situation.

This principal is describing a pervasive attitude in which to many staff members particular children were optional, expendable, and just plain not valued.

Another principal remarked that he worked hard with staff whose attitudes did not match the direction in which he guided the school: "I have teachers who do not want special ed kids in their classroom. They are so worried about these students' behavior. They feel those kids do not have a right to be there." This belief created a school culture in which students in special education were "second-class members of the school community." He asserted, "People don't believe that certain kids—our Black students, our Latino students, our Hmong students, our students with disabilities—can do better." He believed that this pervasive attitude impeded a great deal of his social justice work. He described it as an "acceptance of failure and mediocrity for the students of color, students learning English, and students with special needs." This principal felt that over time many staff had slowly moved away from these beliefs.

The principals felt that they continually struggled with the attitudes held by some staff members who did not want to take at least some responsibility for their students not learning and did not want to be reflective about changing their practice. They did believe that they saw these attitudes changing slowly and with at least some people. However, they discerned formidable resistance from obstructive staff attitudes.

The literature on leading for equity and social justice sheds light on this type of countervailing pressure to seeking social change. Skrla et al. (2004) reported that the general lack of understanding that school staffs maintain about the present levels of inequity acts as a barrier to social justice. This ignorance of present-day inequities was compounded by even well-intentioned staff who treat "differences as deficits, a process that locates the responsibility for school success in the lived experience of children (home life, home culture, SES [socioeconomic status]) rather than situating responsibility in the education system. . . . [They] assign blame for school failure to children and to their families" (p. 114). This lack of understanding and deficit-oriented thinking was complicated by school staffs wanting to ignore issues of race (Bell, Jones, & Johnson, 2002; Skrla et al., 2004; Solomon, 2002), poverty (Lyman & Villani, 2002), and sexual orientation (Capper et al., 2006) because it is impossible to discuss equity and social justice changes in diverse schools without understanding and discussing the intersection of these critical social identities. The combination of factors presented in the literature helps put the obstructive staff attitudes found by the principals into perspective. What I found from these leaders concurs with the literature on equity and social justice, in that staff attitudes and beliefs can apply significant pressure and resistance. Parent and community expectations and attitudes also led to serious pressure against these principals' efforts to create more just schools.

Parental Expectations

The final location of barriers from the school site to social justice was insular or privileged parental expectations. "A community battle, that's a piece that you can't leave out when you're talking about equity work. That's been the most challenging piece of my work," stated one principal while discussing the barriers she faced to her social justice agenda. The seven principals cited parental expectations and community attitudes when they discussed the barriers. I provide three representative examples. Again, in this section I do not use pseudonyms.

One principal in a sizeable middle income and affluent community had numerous tough experiences with a portion of the school community that held

> a certain expectation, a certain viewpoint on entitlement and privilege, and it's made very clear to me. . . . During the class placement process a family who I knew was affluent and well connected in the community directly confronted me. There was no space in a particular classroom and I was told outright [by this family] that it was my job to kick out a student, whose parent was not advocating for them, and then move that other child to another classroom so I could add their child. Wow! That was a whole lot of entitlement right there.

This example reveals how the principals described that certain families felt that their children's education needed to be the foremost priority for the school, at the expense of other students. The example is clearly not subtle in how this family articulated their sense of entitlement. The principal offered another example of this type of parental expectation while detracking their math program:

> [A group of parents] who have always been very aggressive about that they want things done a certain way and want their desires met . . . threatened me and my job and my position. . . . [The parents said to me,] "If this doesn't happen our way, there are going to be consequences." They were threatening my job and reputation. It wasn't a bluff, they had done it before with other principals and had really hurt these other administrators emotionally and professionally.

This was another overt example of how these principals describe an empowered group of parents demanding their way and in this case opposing equity-based reform. As the principals challenged inequitable norms, such as a tracked system that was clearly benefiting some "privileged" families over marginalized families, particular families acted as barriers.

Another principal commented that there was definitely an attitude from some active White parents that "my kid's needs come first," and "I expect the school to make what I want to happen a reality for my kid." This principal felt that even in cases in which the White, middle-class, active families did embrace the diversity of the community, this was accompanied by a sense of charity and not a commitment to justice or change. The feeling of many of the active White parents was, "My kid's needs come first, and we will value helping/giving a handout to the 'poor' students, not changing barriers to their success; we value charity, not equity." This principal continued,

> At least once a month White parents came to my office and said, "I'm not racist, but I'm worried about what's happening in my child's classroom. I don't want to blame it on the African American and Latino kids." Without exception, the parent would then blame whatever the issue was on an African American or Latino kid. While I do not deny that there were sometimes real issues to be concerned about in some classrooms, in general the students of the parents who were in my office were getting an excellent education.

The fact that this was a recurring parental behavior made this barrier feel all the more powerful, as this principal was the only one who could see this racially biased pattern. One of the principals summarized this dilemma and struggle clearly: "It's basically the belief that one is entitled to certain privileges, and it's very difficult to work with that and to make sure that school is equitable for all." The principals felt that such attitudes and beliefs impeded the equity work they were trying to enact.

Particular parents' acting as barriers to a social justice agenda is discussed in the literature. Oakes et al. (2000) found that families who benefited from the inequities of the status quo created significant resistance to change, even if the changes brought greater equity. Brown (2004) argued that entrenched beliefs in society and, in turn, families valued traditional and technical leadership, and Vibert and Portelli (2002) concurred that innovative leadership has not been valued. These beliefs, along with incomprehension among middle-class and affluent families about present-day inequities (Skrla et al., 2004), the White community's desire to ignore race (Bell et al., 2002; Skrla et al., 2004; Solomon, 2002), and middle- to upper-income families' disinterest in issues of poverty (Lyman & Villani, 2002) create significant barriers and countervailing pressure that the principals felt from some of their families.

Scholars whose work is not centered on leadership for equity or justice have also contributed to understanding parental pressure against social justice reform. Kohn (1998) found that affluent White parents

> ignore everyone else's children, focusing their efforts solely on giving their own children the most desirable education. . . . They are in effect sacrificing other children to their own. . . . It is not enough for their kids to win: others must lose—and they must lose conspicuously. (p. 570)

Brantlinger, Majd-Jabbari, and Guskin (1996) studied White middle-class mothers who "wanted to perceive themselves—and be perceived—as liberals who were just and compassionate people" (p. 586). These liberal mothers said they valued "socially inclusive, integrated ideals of education" (p. 589), but through their actions they "were intent on having advantaged circumstances for their own children" (p. 589). The seven leaders, like authors of the literature, found that privileged parents could create tremendous pressure against a social justice agenda.

In sum, these principals confronted barriers at their schools in response to their attempts to make equity-oriented changes: The vast scope of the principalship and intense personal pressures created unceasing resistance to advancing social justice. While the scope of the position generates pressure for all principals, the additional layers of work and turmoil caused by seeing injustice embedded in their schools, feeling a responsibility to "fix it," and then working to change the injustice results in particular resistance. School norms, staff attitudes, and particular families created other significant barriers to the pursuit of equity and justice. Barriers put up by the school district and at the institutional level compounded these pressures.

BARRIERS AT THE DISTRICT LEVEL

The second location that produced barriers to the principals' social justice agenda was at the district level. The principals felt that forces from outside the school and local community played a significant role in obstructing their reform efforts. The principals described three areas of resistance that came from the district: a formidable bureaucracy, unsupportive central office administrators, and unimaginative fellow principals.

Formidable Bureaucracy

One means by which forces from the district caused resistance to social justice work was a formidable bureaucracy. All the principals worked in sizable districts and felt that the district bureaucracy impeded their progress in enacting equity. Principal Eli continually felt the bureaucracy provided pressure counter to his agenda. This high school principal felt the system itself did not promote equity and justice:

> The culture of bureaucracy is not set up to support this; reporting structures are very confusing, very blurred. You don't know who you report to, who has got the power over you, and they all give you directives. . . . [We're expected] to have better bulletin boards, better minutes of meetings. More meetings, better minutes, that kind of stuff. . . . You run into bureaucrats who tell you you can't do things. . . . You need to have this form on yellow, not blue, paper. . . . It's about compliance with the bureaucracy, but the bureaucracy is not about issues of equity.

Principal Eli felt resistance from the structure of the organization and the minutiae of demands and expectations that were a part of the school system. While these demands were placed on everyone regardless of social justice commitment, they took away time and energy from his social justice agenda.

Principal Natalie felt pressure and frustration from the institutional expectation that the entire district move in one direction about certain issues at the same time:

> Not allowing us to take the next step, making sure that we're all "in step together" is difficult. Being arrogant, I'm saying that our school is beyond some of these other schools. I'm saying that our staff truly as an entire staff believes they don't know everything. Our staff truly believes that they want to make things better, they want to take the next step, but being held back and saying, "We're all doing this together," or "You're going to mess up everything," is difficult for us as a staff. That's a real distinct struggle right now.

She felt this resistance in regard to issues that she had already addressed with her staff that were part of district initiatives. In this case this district initiative to examine equity was a part of Principal Natalie's vision for her high school, but the fact that the whole school district was approaching it together in the same way at the same time slowed down her social justice agenda, as she and her staff had already moved past where the district was beginning.

Principal Dale articulated how the bureaucracy acted as a barrier for him:

> We are getting more and more urgent requests from central office. It doesn't have that sort of physical note attached saying, "How much additional work is that going to cause the principal and others?" . . . We get these sort of urgent notices: "You need to reply within a week, telling us how many kids are involved in this," or a report on this . . . but I think they don't recognize the complexity of school life.

Like Principal Eli, Principal Dale perceived a constant barrage of urgent work to keep the bureaucracy running that took away time from his middle school agenda. In sum, these principals encountered resistance and pressure to deviate from their agenda that they attributed to the bureaucracy but they also felt resistance from individual central office administrators.

In the literature on organizations, Herriott and Firestone (1984) described bureaucracy as having a "single set of goals. . . . Top administrators translate general goals into tasks to be implemented" (p. 42). Since educational administration has not traditionally been focused on social justice (Bell et al., 2002; Brown, 2004; Lyman & Villani, 2002; Marshall, 2004; Pohland & Carlson, 1993; Rapp, 2002; Rusch, 2004; Solomon, 2002) and since leaders who seek equity and justice are labeled negatively (Bogotch, 2002; Dantley, 2002) and not valued (Vibert & Portelli, 2002), it makes sense that the principals in this study ran into barriers within the bureaucracy, because they maintained their own goals of equity and justice and not necessarily the single set of the bureaucracy. The bureaucracy also acts as a barrier in that both organizational structure and processes maintain divisions that inhibit communication and "prevent [those within the bureaucracy] from sharing their strengths" (Ghosal & Bartlett, 1995, p. 88). The seven principals experienced barriers from the bureaucracy that the literature helps to explain.

Unsupportive Central Office Administrators

Unsupportive central office administrators were a significant source of resistance. Specific people in the central offices of these urban districts acted either knowingly or unknowingly as resistant forces to the principals' efforts. All seven principals identified specific people or instances generating resistance from the central office. I provide two examples from these principals' experiences, again not using pseudonyms, to offer a protective distance for the principals in their sharing sensitive stories.

One principal had an experience with a supervisor who mandated high school scheduling and course changes at the last minute that created enormous amounts of work for no meaningful purpose.

> I got written up by one of my superiors because he claimed I violated the directives. . . . There was a very unclear description about what courses kids had to take as a freshman. . . . According to the regulations you only need 2 years of gym, so for a variety of pretty thoughtful and academic reasons, we were not going to have gym during freshman year. Well, he told me, after the school year started, "You've got to have freshmen take gym." So we had to redo all these schedules, programs, and all this extra work took away planning time for teachers. We almost lost a teacher, who was so frustrated with this just so we could do what my supervisor wanted, and it wasn't really the law. . . . He wrote a discipline memo to me that is now in my personnel file at the school system office.

This principal gave an example of the frustration and extra work caused by a central office administrator. This specific action is not directly about advocating for his marginalized students and could have happened to any principal. The principal regards this as a barrier to his social justice work for a number of reasons. First, as discussed previously, the enormity of the job puts a strain on the amount of time and energy available for tackling the larger social justice issues, and redoing the schedule exacerbated that issue. Second, part of this principal's agenda was to empower teachers in the running of the school, which was clearly not accomplished during this situation, as evidenced by the resentment and frustration expressed by one of the teachers. Indeed, the principal felt he was wasting the teachers' time as a result of this directive from the central office administrator. Third, he chose to comply with his supervisor's demands instead of resisting, which actually compounded his own feelings of resistance because ultimately he was still "written up" for his actions. He received disciplinary measures for a situation in which he compromised what he felt was best in order to work within the system. As a result, he was labeled as a troublemaker, and was labeled that way for a "fairly insignificant issue."

Another principal felt constant condescension from one of the assistant superintendents who worked in the central office. This principal took a 3-week leave for the birth of his child. During his absence, a 30-year veteran and retired principal acted as a replacement. The principal described their subsequent conversation:

> When I came back, John [the retired principal] sat me down and said, "Wow, this is a busy place. This school is completely different than it used to be when I worked at [the middle school fed by this elementary school]. There are lots of great things happening *now*. But I have to tell you, I am

exhausted. I need to tell Vanessa [the assistant superintendent] about my experience here. She needs to know what a great job you are doing and how hard I had to work to keep up with all you are doing." I was taken aback but appreciated his praise.

This principal remarked that later that school year, he went to meet with Vanessa, the assistant superintendent, about resources for the following year. He recalled that interaction:

Vanessa brought up what John said and told me, "If you had put in place better structures, John would not have had to work that hard. I will give you time to go to other schools to see how they handle things." I was shocked and appalled. There was a lot to do at my school because I felt we were doing things differently, making real change, and treating kids more humanely. Vanessa wanted to send me to schools that have "naughty rooms," "in-school suspension rooms," and "segregated special education rooms." I did not need to go visit the schools she suggested to see how they segregate and warehouse all the naughty [kids] and kids of color. I was working so hard to move my school away from those practices. I was angry and hurt. To me this was such a devaluing of the kinds of equity and social justice work that was needed in my school and in many schools in our district.

The progress this principal made at his school was clearly neither understood nor recognized by the district office, and it seems as though it was being undermined. These principals felt direct resistance from central office administrators to their equity and justice agenda.

Central office administrators' resistance to the principals' drive to enact social justice is also described in the literature on leadership. It is known that traditional and technical leadership is most valued (Brown, 2004), innovative leaders are not respected (Vibert & Portelli, 2002), leaders with a passion for enacting justice have been treated as incompetent (Touchton & Acker-Hocevar, 2001), these leaders are often labeled negatively (Bogotch, 2002; Dantley, 2002), and there remains a lack of understanding of present levels of inequities (Skrla et al., 2004). Given that, it is not surprising that the principals encountered resistance from central office administrators. The literature on leadership for equity and social justice gives examples of how district administration causes resistance to advancing social change efforts, but does not directly address central office administrators being ongoing barriers to this work. I position the collection of examples these principals offered as part of the persistent resistance to social justice. The principals discussed not only specific administrators but also their principal colleagues as barriers to this work.

Prosaic Administrator Colleagues

Prosaic, or unimaginative, colleagues were the third barrier that came from the district level. The principals divulged that their colleagues, both principals and other administrators, put up resistance to advancing justice and equity in schools. They defined prosaic colleagues to mean the majority of their fellow principals and peer administrators. The seven principals believed that these colleagues had neither the drive, commitment, or knowledge to carry out an equity-oriented school reform agenda nor the belief that they should. As a high school principal, Eli noted frequent frustration in his principal colleagues. He stated:

> It's depressing. Most [principals] are 15- to 20-year veterans of school systems. They're tired, they're tired of the classroom, they want to make more money, and they want to have to a certain degree of power over other people. That's why they wanted to become principals. . . . Very few of them, if you ask them why they're doing this, will talk about creating high schools that really serve and respect kids. . . . They're just technically very adept but they have no sense of passion or vision for equity.

As an elementary principal, Tracy realized that justice and equity was not what many of his administrator colleagues were worrying about:

> They were not losing sleep over issues of race, language, or disability. . . . Many of my colleagues were not getting things done in terms of access for students with disabilities or tackling issues around race, discipline, and student learning. As I learned more about their schools and their school plans for the future, it seemed like certain things were not happening at their schools: Achievement gaps were not closing, pullout or tracked programs were perpetuated, tough kids were still being seen as criminals, their schools were not inviting places, and lots of things were not getting better.

He continued,

> That was hugely frustrating because as a group of principals we spent all our time together talking about other stuff and having meetings and planning initiatives that really had no chance of making a big difference. . . . We never got to the point where justice was about anything more than what I did alone quietly at my school.

Principal Tracy felt isolated and supported by only a few colleagues who had the knowledge and passion for equity issues as well as the language to engage in substantial conversation around these topics and implications for schools, structures, practices, curriculum and instruction.

The institutional expectation that the entire district move in one direction acted as a district level barrier to Principal Natalie, and she felt that her secondary colleagues were not "keeping pace":

> Some of these other leaders just don't know how to get their staffs moving or how to tackle even the most surface equity issues that the district is finally examining. But I am being held back because "we're all doing this together" or "you're going to mess up everything by moving too fast." Constantly being told that when we are ahead of the curve is difficult for me and for my staff. That's a real distinct struggle.

This barrier came from the district's attempt to look at equity issues that Principal Natalie felt she had moved her staff beyond. She was not critical of the district tackling these issues; she felt penalized or reprimanded because her principal colleagues were not capable of dealing with or had not tackled these equity issues already.

These leaders for social justice continued to do their work despite the resistance, pressure, and frustration they felt as a result of their administrator colleagues. They discussed that this pressure not only affected their personal work, it also limited space for equity at a district or larger level. While the literature on social justice leadership does not directly propose that principals and other administrators who do not possess the drive or determination to advance equity and justice act as barriers to this work, these principals' realities resonate in the literature in two ways. First, the feelings they expressed related to the isolation and lack of support from their principal colleagues were partially explained by the fact that the field of educational administration has not traditionally embraced social justice and leading for social justice has not been central to preparing administrators (Bell et al., 2002; Brown, 2004; Cambron-McCabe & McCarthy, 2005; Lyman & Villani, 2002; Marshall, 2004; Pohland & Carlson, 1993; Rapp, 2002; Rusch, 2004; Solomon, 2002). Second, many of the principals' colleagues had a tendency to ignore issues of race (Bell et al., 2002; Skrla et al., 2004; Solomon, 2002), did not understand issues of poverty (Lyman & Villani, 2002), and clearly lacked awareness of the current inequities that existed in schools (Skrla et al., 2004). The ways in which these principals described resistance from their colleagues corroborates conclusions that leadership scholars have previously asserted. However, the principals not only substantiate these conclusions as the realities, they also describe how the realities exist and become formidable resistance to seeking equity and justice.

While some of the ways the district level manifested resistance for the principals here also affects principals who do not have a justice orientation, the barriers have particular implications for SJL. For example, many principals receive resistance from central office administrators or are frustrated by a large bureaucracy, but enacting social justice in systems not set up to support this work, under supervisors who do not understand or value the work, and alongside colleagues who lack the knowledge and passion to do the work, results in distinct barriers for the principals who come to the field to lead for social justice. The frustration and barriers these principals described about the bureaucracy, central office administrators, and other principals are not simply the typical complaints that many people share about supervisors and co-workers. Their words depict ongoing resistance to achieve equity and justice alongside supervisors and colleagues who, according to one principal in the study, "just don't get it. They don't understand justice and they don't work for equity."

BARRIERS AT THE INSTITUTIONAL LEVEL

The final aspect of the organization that set up barriers to the principals' social justice agenda came at the institutional level—at both the policy and university levels. The principals described three types of barriers that came from the institutional level: a lack of resources, harmful state and federal regulations, and principal preparation.

Lack of Resources

The first way that these principals encountered barriers from the institutional level was through a lack of resources. Three examples are provided about principals' feeling squeezed by "insufficient resources." Principal Tracy described a particular tension with this issue. He placed the issue of "insufficient resources" within the context of a ritual developed with fifth graders—"Potter with the Principal." He would read and discuss the widely popular Harry Potter books with the fifth grade. He described this:

> As the Harry Potter movies came out it was clear that many young people from suburban and more affluent communities were going to experience the thrill of the release of the Harry Potter movies together with their classes, school, and/or friends. To me this was an issue again dividing kids and families by income. . . . I spent time finding money and fund-raising to take the entire fifth grade to *Harry Potter* at the time of the movie release so all of my fifth graders could have this experience regardless of income or privilege. I found a donor. But it came back to the fact that I had to find or beg for resources. In order to provide this equitable experience, and a relatively small and insignificant one at that, it took a fair amount of effort and time, which took away from other important work.

While this principal, as well as many of the other principals, were able to raise hundreds of thousands of dollars for various important projects, the fact remained that they had to expend vast amounts of time and energy just to stay afloat. This ultimately took away from their time and ability to focus on curriculum and structural and human resource issues related to equity and justice.

Principal Natalie felt that a lack of resources impeded her social justice work with high school staff in a different way:

> Money is always a barrier, and time. . . . there's never enough money for staff development, or time for it either. I'd love to give the staff some more time to prepare and learn by reading these books we are working on like *Why Are All the Black Kids Sitting Together in the Cafeteria?* [Tatum, 1997], *From Rage to Hope* [Kuykendall, 1991], *No Excuses* [Carter, 2000]. And we need more staff development money to help teachers prepare to change their teaching [and] their curriculum and to differentiate their curriculum.

She felt that with the "almost laughable" small amount of time in the yearly calendar—worked out between the school district and the teachers union—devoted to staff development, she could not facilitate, encourage, or expect the kind of learning her staff needed and wanted. The amount of money she had to use for professional development for her entire school staff "would not even buy lunch at a private or corporate training." While some educators take pride in being able to stretch a small amount of resources (these leaders included), the principals positioned some of the resources at their disposal as insufficient to do the job appropriately and to facilitate equity across society. Principal Eli echoed that sentiment for his high school:

> We never have enough materials! We were given hardly any textbooks, no computers, raggedy furniture. . . . What frustrates me is you get the lowest-performing kids in your neighborhood with inadequate facilities, inadequate funding. . . . You want to be able to do good work, you want to have at least some of the tools needed to do this work. You want at least some of the resources these kids deserve. That gets me angry.

These principals identified instances when a lack of resources created serious pressure against their drive to enact justice. While they maintained their struggle to create more equitable schools, they viewed the ways resources were provided to their urban schools as inequitable and insufficient. They understood that a lack of resources hurt every school, but they believed it hit marginalized students hardest.

Scholars have explored how a resource deficit creates barriers to social justice. Kozol (1991, 1996, 2000, 2005) paints a grim picture of the graphic economic disparities that marginalized students face in their classroom and schools. Court cases such as *Williams* in California or *Fiscal Equity* in New York reflect the inequitable resources the principals in this book describe. The lack of resources that these students endure works to maintain an inequitable education system. Further, Kinney (2003) and Erickson (2004) report on ever tightening public school budgets. The barriers raised by a lack of resources are depicted in Kozol's work on the economic inequities faced by schools serving marginalized students, as is the shrinking pool of resources for all schools.

State and Federal Regulations

State and federal regulations were the second way in which forces from the institutional level created barriers to advancing social justice. The principals cited specific regulations placed on them by state and the federal governments that created resistance. Principal Scott described how state regulations compromised his ability to increase access, improve the teaching and curriculum, and create a climate of belonging:

> Our state legislature has created funding policies for schools that have drained our district of significant resources. We have been forced to cut tens of millions of dollars each year for years now. School after school has had assistant principals cut; the special-ed-teacher-to-student ratio has steadily risen; class size has gotten steadily bigger; social workers, counselors, music programs, [and] librarians are becoming dangerously scarce. These funding policies have dramatically impacted what I can accomplish on my [social justice] agenda. But what bothers me the most is that the most vulnerable students have been impacted the most by these cuts.

Principal Scott felt that while reductions in school funding may have affected all schools in his state, they had a heightened impact on the ability to create more equitable and just norms. This relates to the previous section on the lack of resources, but also to the fact that the cuts have a greater impact on providing access to music, library media, and social workers, which has a disparate effect on students from low-income families compared with their more affluent peers. This undercuts what these principals were trying to provide for their students.

Principal Tracy discussed No Child Left Behind and explained that he was not sure that labeling schools as "failing" did any good—for a couple of reasons that people do not usually talk about:

By labeling the school as failing, it sends a message to parents and staff that this school was not working. We know from research and from public opinion surveys that most people feel that *their* school is a *good* school. Our community was the same way. While serious improvement was needed at our school, labeling our school as failing created unproductive dissonance. For some White parents and teachers it again became about blaming the Black kids or the poor kids or the kids with disabilities. For some parents of color, it sounded like, "I have a good kid, what's wrong with those White teachers?"

That sort of blaming did not help his school or community. In this example, not only did the school need significant improvement in terms of curriculum and instruction, this principal needed to mend all the wounds that were opened by being labeled a "failure." It is important to understand the context of Principal Tracy's comments. When he began as principal, his school was put on the state's list of schools in need of improvement. When he arrived, only 70% of the students were evaluated on state and local assessment. Three years later, 98% participated in assessments. When he started, roughly 50% of the students achieved proficient or advance levels in reading; this rose to 86%. All groups of students showed significant gains: African American students improved from 33% to 78%, Latino students improved from 18% to 100%, Asian students improved from 47% to 100%, students with disabilities improved from 13% to 60%, ELL students improved from 17% to 100%, and students in poverty improved from 40% to 78%.

He continued with the second reason he was skeptical about the label "failing schools." As schools continue to "fail," the teachers and principal lose more and more control over the operations of the school. In Principal Tracy's district and state the longer a school was on the state list of schools in need of improvement the more control the school lost. First the district officials would take over the running of the school and then the state would take over. He shared his position:

> I knew these district administrators and state officials personally and I had worked with them for years and for the most part they are good folks but had no idea how to lead a "failing" school to a better place. In fact, when two of them, one current assistant superintendent and one state official, left the principalship after many years to move to their new positions, they left their schools on the list of schools needing improvement. So I wonder, if they did not lead the schools they were charged with to a better place, how did we expect them to be able to tell me how to lead mine?

While aspects of the No Child Left Behind Act align under the surface with these leaders' convictions to better serve children who historically and currently receive a marginal education, Principal Tracy felt this federal law as well as other regulations acted as barriers.

State and federal regulations created a significant resistance to the principals' work to advance social justice. From how schools were funded to federal education acts, specific policies frustrated these justice-oriented principals.

Scheurich, Skrla, and Johnson (2000) and Skrla et al. (2004) described both the positive and negative effects that accountability policies and No Child Left Behind have on advancing equity in public schools. They explained that advances toward and retreats away from social justice happen in the wake of these policies and argued that critiquing No Child Left Behind and other accountability policies is not enough in advancing justice, but that it is imperative to focus both research and practice on how to seize this moment in history to make equity a reality.

Additionally, school policy and funding are written about and discussed frequently in education research and in the popular media. Critiques of No Child Left Behind have taken an increasing prominent place in educational literature (American Educational Research Association [AERA], 2004, 2005, 2006, 2007, 2008) and educational discussions. School funding takes a prominent place in scholarly work (AERA, 2004, 2005, 2006, 2007) as well as in the media. The principals' frustrations with specific policies are echoed throughout the scholarly and popular educational literature.

Principal Preparation

The final source from where these principals found barriers to advancing social justice came from the uninspired preparation that they had received. The principals saw their principal preparation programs as being barriers to advancing social justice. Again, no names or pseudonyms are used in this section to maintain further confidentiality. One principal stated, "My preparation program really didn't light the fire, it didn't help [with equity issues]." While he used a lot of what he learned in one class on inclusive schooling, he felt "it's a joke to talk about more classes like the principalship." He felt a disconnect between what he needed to do to advance equity and what he learned in his principal preparation. In discussing content and instruction about equity and justice in the preparation program, this principal said, "Equity and justice in my preparation program? None, nothing. I'm afraid there was nothing."

"I don't think that race and equity were ever addressed directly in my administrative training," commented another principal. She discussed her programs focus: "It was more management, yeah, more management. I don't think we ever talked about issues of justice or even how justice fits into management." The principals agreed that while there was content related to effective leadership and administrator skills, they gained "nothing" about how to be social justice leaders, "nothing" about how to use equity as a lens and the ways equity and justice are interrelated to so many aspects of leadership and schools.

Another principal remarked,

> I feel that a lot of the preparation was theoretical, but not theory about equity or race or dealing with the big issues. It was bland, like the "4-frames" or generic community relations or school business without any lenses about bigger issues and it all lacked substance. . . . Part of the problem [with my administrator preparation] was that I was taught by a bunch of really smart people, but most of them had never been school administrators and the few that had been had no understanding of equity issues. So while I respected their knowledge and intellect, none of them could really talk [about leading for social justice] in anything but abstract ways. They're really smart but most of them don't really get it. They don't understand the realities of school leadership focused on equity.

This principal was frustrated that the content of the preparation program was generic and unrelated to equity and justice issues, but also she felt that the faculty lacked credibility because most of the faculty in her program were never administrators. While she and the other principals never questioned the university faculty's intellect, they articulated they felt a lack of content relating to equity and justice issues and a lack of faculty practical experience in creating more equitable schools.

These principals felt frustrated at the lack of learning opportunities to support justice in their principal preparation programs. While they individually possessed a drive to do justice work, they felt unsupported by their graduate studies in educational administration. They felt their programs maintained the understanding that administration was not about leading for justice. Not only were learning opportunities in this area omitted, but also principal training seemed more geared toward less passionate leaders without the skills or motivation to do this work.

The growing body of work on leadership for social justice supports these principals' assertions that their preparation programs did not support their desire to enact equity and that the preparation programs were not focused on issues of social justice (Bell et al., 2002; Brown, 2004; Lyman & Villani, 2002; Marshall, 2004; Pohland & Carlson, 1993; Rapp, 2002; Rusch, 2004; Solomon, 2002). These leaders experienced strong congruence with the literature on social justice leadership in the area of principal preparation.

CONSEQUENCES OF THE BARRIERS

The principals felt that the result of the barriers was serious consequences for them. Six out of the seven described a great personal toll and all seven described a persistent sense of discouragement as a result of the ongoing, harsh, and relentless resistance they faced. The principals candidly detailed the serious toll on their bodies, their emotions, and their lives.

One principal asserted that the resistance "eats away at who you are. It's relentless and it caused serious depression. My vision for kids and for schools has been maintained, but I feel beat up, I feel like I am never going to make it. I feel like I am never going to be the same."

Another principal commented that working more than 60 hours a week "really is physically and emotionally exhausting as a leader." She explained:

> There are so many battles to fight and there are so many obstacles to my work [for equity and justice]. . . . I'm exhausted, my body aches, my soul feels wilted. . . . I knew being the kind of principal I wanted to be would not be easy, but I had no idea I would be tormented in this way. . . . I need to say again that my whole entire [starting to cry] value system has been questioned.

A third principal explained that the kinds of hours and dedication his social justice leadership requires was

> endangering my health and my family. I am rarely home; I am always consumed by all the problems, the big problems, not the day-to-day stuff. . . . I would be lying if I said my health and my well-being were not suffering. I am gaining weight and losing sleep and drinking [alcohol] more. I wake up at all hours of the night with my mind racing about what I need to do. It is all-consuming.

The fourth principal discussed the toll and discouragement together. After working 60 to 70 hours a week,

> some days, I don't feel I've done anything right. . . . Emotionally there's a lot that builds up and emotionally you want to make everybody's life OK, but you can't do that all the time, and that's a stress. . . . There's so much, and when a deadline happens, it means putting in more early morning time or night time, taking away from personal time, so I don't let a kid down. This toll is going to be on me. . . . It's an emotional roller coaster around here [laughs]; it really is, it really is. . . . It's been really tough [voice breaking], really tough.

The fifth principal was so tormented by the fact he could not change things fast enough that his frustration ate him up physically and emotionally. When all the pressures came together, and his school was not better fast enough, it just drove him "crazy." He confided:

There were periods of months when I vomited every morning. There were periods of time when every day I would cry alone in my office because I could see the pain that was being inflicted on kids. As the principal, I was ultimately responsible for that pain, but also I could see the reality was that I could not change it fast enough. That took a huge toll on who I was. I had trouble sleeping. I would lose 30 pounds and gain it back, lose 20 pounds and gain it back. This work kept crushing my spirit. That might have been the hardest to take. I did not feel like I was the same person I had been before. I would drink alcohol more and more. I sought mental health counseling. I wondered, Who am I? What happened to me?

Another principal said that working 10 to 11 hours a day, plus every weekend morning and most days over the summer, made the job and the need to enact justice "all-consuming."

[I] felt a personal toll, when I see the kids' situations. They are not getting what they deserve and our society is letting them down time and time again. I wonder if we are doing any good. I feel the intense drive to make their education better, but I feel like there is so much up against this work. Am I doing any good?

One more principal articulated the sense of persistent discouragement:

[Working toward social justice] is incredibly hard work; I do not think people understand how hard this is. . . . And it is so discouraging. There is so much to do; there are enormous problems with the current reality. And you feel the need to make it better and you need it to be better fast, but it is too much. I see all the work that still needs to be done and I think, I can't do this, I am no good. I am a total f-up.

These leaders articulated the stress, frustration, and pain that they felt because of the ongoing barriers they faced. This toll deeply affected them. While they had achieved significant accomplishments, they felt defeated and questioned if they could do this job. They maintained a commitment to their vision of equity and justice, but they indicated that maintaining that vision came at a price.

The barriers to enacting justice clearly became a burden for the social justice principals. This burden took a significant toll on these leaders, their bodies, and their emotional well-being. How measurable this toll was varies, but three principals described serious chronic medical issues they and their doctors at least partially attributed to the stress of their positions. Two have had marital/relationship struggles in part because of their work. Four sought mental health professional support in relation to the barriers to their work, and three were "overlooked" or denied promotion in their districts. I feel an obligation to position the struggle to advance social justice within the principals' experiences of pain. These leaders described the resistance they faced and were candid about the toll and discouragement they felt as a result of that resistance.

CONCLUSION

The barriers discussed here to advancing social justice is prevalent in many schools in the United States, and many leaders who are not necessarily social justice oriented face these barriers in their school improvement efforts. All principals face barriers and encounter significant pressure in their position, and some of the barriers reported here are found in every school that is changing and seeking school improvement. However, the barriers detailed in this chapter differ from those in typical schools and for typical school leaders in a number of ways. First, the work of these social justice leaders was quite personal. They were passionately committed to social justice and their success in advancing social justice is at their very core; thus resistance becomes personal and attacks not only their work but also who they are.

Also, their work to advance social justice directly challenged both the deficit thinking and the privilege that permeates schools and communities. Other school improvement efforts not necessarily directed at advancing social justice, such as adopting a block schedule, changing lunchtimes, or using a specific math curriculum, can result in significant staff and community resistance. However, such school improvements do not ultimately challenge two ingrained and often unspoken premises—Certain (privileged) children are entitled to a better education and historically marginalized children cannot reach high academic achievement and should not receive the same curriculum and instruction as their privileged peers. Challenging hegemonic norms produces particular and powerful resistance to the social justice work (Apple, 1996; Rapp, 2002).

Finally, the principals leading for social justice directly defied the meta-narrative that school leaders should be technical bureaucrats (Brown, 2004) and lockstep managers of the status quo (Oakes et al, 2000; Rapp, 2002). The principals brought a commitment to justice through leadership that was passionate, personal, informed about equity, humble, and boundary pushing. These traits produced resistance from other administrators and educational systems that did not value this type of leadership or wholeheartedly support the principals' social justice agenda.

Principals leading for social justice encountered tremendous barriers. These barriers came from every aspect of the position: the job, themselves, their staff, the community, the school norms and structures, district administration, the bureaucracy, colleagues, larger society, state and federal regulations, and their principal preparation programs. They faced unrelenting pressure. They experienced a physical and emotional toll. They carried a sense of persistent discouragement. In the words of Principal Meg, they faced barriers "at every turn."

The barriers "at every turn" and resulting toll and discouragement reflect a reality that the position of principal continues to move in the direction of impossibility. While hope can be found in the significant accomplishments the principals made in creating more just schools, the field of educational administration is charged with three major responsibilities: prepare leaders who are capable of understanding and creating more socially just schools, build resilience in future and current leaders committed to social justice, and work to reduce the resistance to enacting social justice in schools. This call is not a prescription for social justice, but a reminder that there remains a need for school leaders to commit themselves to social justice aims and a growing need to be able to do just that—create more just and equitable schools.

Tough work, but don't our students deserve it?

> C H A P T E R 8

"Saving My Sanity": The Resilience That Leaders Develop to Sustain Justice and Equity

If there is no struggle, there is no progress.

—Frederick Douglass

Even the strongest have their moments of fatigue.

—Friedrich Nietzche

L EADERS COMMITTED to equity and justice recognize that changing historical and current injustice is far from easy work. Given the enormity and relentless nature of the resistance they faced, the principals experienced both professional and personal challenges. To deal with barriers, they employed strategies that developed a resilience that they felt enabled them to sustain their work to create more just and equitable schools.

In returning to the framework of SJL, this chapter focuses on the resilience the principals developed to sustain them both professionally and personally. Its purpose is to build an understanding of the strategies the principals developed to advance social justice in their schools in the face of significant resistance. This describes another key:

Key 7. Sustain oneself professionally and personally.

The seven principals worked to sustain themselves through the development of various strategies, which became an integral part of maintaining their ability to do this work. The principals developed two kinds of strategies: professional and personal. I start with a discussion of the professional strategies, because they involved approaching the work of the principal in different ways. After the professional strategies, I describe the personal coping strategies. While these strategies were not directly tied to the professional responsibilities of the leaders, the impact they had on the leaders' ability to continue working for social justice is undeniable. For each of the strategies I provide a number of representative examples.

PROFESSIONAL STRATEGIES

Professional strategies are defined as approaches the principals used in their jobs to advance their work toward social justice. The strategies involve taking steps to alter their initial understanding of their work. The principals' professional strategies included communicating purposefully and authentically, developing a supportive administrative network, working together for change, keeping their eyes on the prize, prioritizing their work, engaging in professional learning, and building relationships.

Communicate Purposefully and Authentically

The first professional strategy these leaders used to sustain social justice in the face of barriers was communicating purposefully and authentically. Five of the principals discussed how even if they did not make a particular change right away, they felt it necessary to communicate in a manner that rang true to their vision and values. This took various forms, from asking the right questions, to confronting a specific person, to using humor. Using this purposeful and authentic communication created some momentum in the direction of social justice, reaffirmed the principals' beliefs to those around them, and helped the principals feel that even though change may be slow, they did something by speaking their truth.

Principal Taylor explained how she handled a situation involving the central office:

> I decided that I needed to do something because it's not OK to have things happen that directly negatively impact kids. In this instance I really felt that it was going to make a giant impact on the child, so I spent much time coming up with a communication to the superintendent, someone who I rarely have communication with because we have an assistant superintendent. . . . Mainly I ended it that the reason I'm communicating this is because I'm concerned about the impact on my students and staff.

This situation had involved a decision that was taken out of her hands by central office administrators, who had made a decision contrary to what she and his elementary teachers felt was best for a student with an emotional and behavioral disability. Principal Taylor and her staff were advocating for this student to remain at their school in an inclusive setting, and the central office administrators ultimately decided to move this student to another school in a more restrictive setting. Principal Taylor felt that while she might not have been able to make this decision, she could raise important concerns and communicate the issues she saw as key.

Principal Tracy related what happened during the restructuring of services at his elementary school, when people felt extremely tense and frustrated:

So at our next staff meeting, a week or so after things started getting really tense, I said, "You know, we can scrap our agenda . . ." I was really honest about what I understood people were frustrated by, and what I saw as the main problem—people were treating each other poorly and how that was unacceptable. . . . It was like the elephant in the living room, that everybody sees but nobody wants to discuss. . . . This tension felt like potentially a huge derailment but I was really honest, I was direct and then I tried to be really, really supportive about listening, taking what they said seriously, and then doing something with that.

Principal Tracy's strategy to deal openly with the issues that were confronting his staff was another example of authentic communication. Too often educators avoid public conflict, so the underlying issues never get raised or resolved. In this example, a solution was not reached, but the principal facilitated an important conversation.

Principal Scott discussed working with a contentious middle school effectiveness team. While he felt that many staff on the committee opposed the direction he was taking the school in, he used the team meeting as a forum for sharing his values and beliefs. Staff members voiced frustration about being forced to discuss race, special education, inclusion, and discipline. Principal Scott adamantly gave numerous examples to illustrate that the students with whom the school continually struggles are African American kids in special education. So he said, "All of these issues are really about race." He used these meetings as a way to continually bring up his belief that "nobody is going to come and take the students who we struggle with away. We are the only ones. It is our responsibility to find ways to make all of our kids successful. Nobody is going to do it for us."

These principals found that their authentic and purposeful communication allowed them to move in the direction of justice. Even at times when the change they sought seemed impossibly distant, they felt the need to stand up for what they believed was right. This strategy for communication allowed them to continue to work toward larger goals, because they felt at least they had done something. They felt they had not let important issues go without sacrificing the integrity of their beliefs.

Develop a Supportive Administrator Network

The second professional strategy used by the seven involved developing a supportive network of administrators. All seven principals found that this network of supportive administrators was essential in overcoming barriers and resisting pressures counter to their social justice agenda. Their networks provided opportunities to share ideas, emotional support, encouragement, and assistance in problem solving. Principal Taylor described the network he developed:

I'm really using my colleagues as resources. I have a few people who I really feel connected to, and we've made that commitment to each other . . . that at the drop of a dime, if we ever needed any of us, we would just show up, you know, if any of us had a hard meeting, they would just drop stuff and come, because we need that support. We can't just be out there on our own. . . . It's made a huge difference and I think I'm finding myself calling people more often, taking the time to say, I need a minute, I need to bounce this off of somebody, I don't have to make this decision on my own.

Principal Dale developed confidence in a number of colleagues. He would discuss hard issues and he enjoyed the give and take of sharing ideas and solutions to problems. Principal Dale stressed that having a group of people he trusted made the hard work easier:

I think you also rely upon working with other principals . . . [people] who could relate, to share ideas and share procedures and also to engage in problem solving and in a sense operate as a support group. I think I've really come into that more in the last 3 or 4 years.

These principals found that having colleagues they could talk with, colleagues who shared similar ideals, colleagues they could trust, created the needed feeling of support. They purposefully developed and used this network to advance their justice and equity work. Their network helped dissolve the isolation and loneliness that accompanied their struggles. Not only did the networks provide ideas, more important, they fostered encouragement for principals in overcoming the significant barriers they faced.

Work Together for Change

The third proactive strategy was working together for change. All seven principals found that empowering staff and community members became a strategy to sustain and advance justice in the face of barriers. Many set out to create more democratic schools and (as discussed in Chapter 4) created systems that empowered staff. Using these democratic structures then became a strategy for overcoming the resistance to do equity work. This became an interesting phenomenon in that shared decision making and empowering staff became a strategy that these principals evoked to create a sense of ownership in decisions that brought greater buy-in and, in turn, less pressure counter to the justice-oriented decision. The pressure that remained was not directed solely at the principal; instead, the group shared it.

Principals Dale, Taylor, Scott, Tracy, and Meg employed this strategy through giving people who opposed their changes a time and place to voice their concerns.

This honored the feelings of people in opposition, created dialogue, and facilitated the sharing of ideas and information. The principals felt that giving people a chance to speak their mind created an atmosphere of openness, and with that openness staff and community members heard diverse opinions. Even if they disagreed with the outcome, they had the opportunity to participate.

The other component of this strategy entailed shared decision making, which led to stronger support and diffused barriers. Principal Meg discussed how she used this strategy during the restructuring of her elementary school:

> I had more than 85% of the staff's support and I used that to leverage the parents and the community who knew these teachers. I cited them by name—so and so supports this plan. We circulated the petition that the teachers had signed so that the community could see all these people, that they know and love, support this change. . . . It made it so the teachers didn't have to necessarily stand up and defend themselves but that there was a whole laundry list of people who were in support of it. Knowing how to utilize the support or the intelligence of the staff and their experience and their rapport with the community—that really diffused that confrontational time very rapidly.

Principals Eli, Natalie, Taylor, and Tracy all reported a second aspect to the strategy of working together for change. With their trust and shared decision-making structures, they not only empowered staff, but also reduced the resistance they faced and were therefore not alone in shouldering the pressures that worked against their steps toward justice. Principal Tracy discussed how shared decision making became a strategy to overcome the barriers:

> Our representative staff group gave people ownership in big decisions. I never overturned a decision of that group. So when people complained or felt frustrated, everyone knew it was a collective decision. It changed the sentiment from "The administration is screwing things up" to "This was our decision, we have to make it work." . . . [The pressure] didn't always have to fall only on my shoulders. . . . Not only did we make good decisions, but I felt less alone, less drained, and more inspired to do this type of work.

These principals worked with staff and community to create change in their schools. Their efforts to make their schools more democratic became not only an important advancement toward justice, but also a strategy to overcome the barriers to their equity work. One principal expressed a sentiment held by many of these principals: "The collective is really important. . . . the collective can be really powerful" in changing the school and in sustaining this work. In working together with staff and community, the principals focused the agenda, the discussion, and the direction of their school on issues of equity and justice.

Keep Your Eyes on the Prize

The fourth strategy used to sustain justice in the face of barriers was to keep their eyes on the prize. This strategy took various forms across the different schools. Keeping their eyes on the prize included focusing the agenda on equity issues, celebrating success, taking small steps toward justice, and using data. Keeping everyone at school, including themselves, focused on social justice created not only progress in terms of advancements in their agendas, but also gave the principals nourishment to continue in their struggles. Six of the principals discussed using this strategy to overcome the barriers they faced.

When Principal Natalie felt the pressures of high school administration, or when she felt significant resistance, she used this strategy:

> The thing I do is I go into classrooms because then I see clearly what has to happen because it's for the kids' benefit. So I have staff saying, We don't want academic rigor; I go in the classroom and I think about what's best for these kids. . . . When I am struggling internally, I talk to the kids, I listen to the kids in order to keep telling myself I'm on the right track, because I've got staff telling me that this school has never done this before and this is not what we're about. I hear that, but what's best for the people we're dealing with? And I go back to the kids.

Principal Taylor maintained her focus by asking the hard questions, even if there was not an opportunity to make changes. She felt it was important to ask questions that centered on issues of equity:

> Our building team . . . is the team which determines how to support kids who are struggling. . . . The last step could be referral for special education. . . . We just noticed that many of the recommendations [to the team] were all Black students, Black male students, and the question I asked [was], "Would this be a recommendation if it was a White child?" And you know, obviously that's a very difficult question for a teacher to answer. I know in the meeting it was very difficult, but I still asked the question . . . but the reaction, it was a hard reaction, it was a difficult reaction . . . but that teacher actually came back to me a couple days later and said to me, "You know that question came at me and you could probably tell by my reaction that I was somewhat offended and a little upset," . . . and she said, "You know in the last couple days I actually have thought about it and here's what I think." So in the long run I think that a

lot of the questions helped each of us to reflect a little bit deeper . . . not necessarily changing our decisions in some situations but making us think.

Principal Meg also infused discussions about elementary school improvement, discipline, and student achievement with issues of race. She explained, "Knowing that I did one small thing in the midst of the daily discord can allow me to sleep at night. When I feel the successes of even small accomplishments, it fuels me to keep going."

By keeping their eyes on the prize—student success, staff success, and tangible indicators of social justice—the principals fostered momentum at their schools to keep issues of social justice at the heart of their collective consciousness. This momentum aided in creating a more just school by changing the norms to include issues of social justice. Additionally, keeping their eyes on the prize allowed the principals to feel they made at least small steps toward their agenda. This feeling helped sustain them personally to further this justice work.

Prioritize Your Work

The fifth strategy the seven principals used as a form of resilience was to prioritize their work. All seven principals used this strategy to keep from going "crazy" but also to make time to do the justice work they felt needed to be done. Principal Eli shared his views on compromising and prioritizing. This approach, he believed, helped him to sustain his momentum and make inroads toward justice at his high school:

> You've got to pick and choose; you don't want to be a martyr for the cause. You don't mind being a martyr for something real important. I'd die on my sword for something really important. . . . I'm not going to die on my sword because some bureaucrat wrote a memo criticizing me. I'm not going to quit my job or get distracted saying they're assholes, or whatever. No, you've got to be smart, you've got to know what you want to accomplish, and you know when to jump through hoops, when to stand up for things. . . . You have to bite your tongue and think before you say and act.

In discussing how he prioritized his work at his middle school, Principal Scott said:

> [I learned to] ignore some of the work. . . . Very few principals get everything that they're supposed to do, and even the ones that do may or may not be considered effective. People consider principals effective when the school, the school is running smoothly. I guess I don't

know for sure why, but principals keep their jobs sometimes even if they don't get all the paperwork done. Principals are beloved even if lots of work isn't getting done.

This realization allowed him a little relief from the constant pressure he felt was contrary to his equity-and-justice agenda.

Principal Taylor prioritized by delegating responsibilities and cultivating leaders among her elementary staff:

> I've got a lot of leaders and I give them a lot of responsibility. I also bring leadership out of people, people who have never had that responsibility. I have two really quiet people; they're my leaders this year because they've stepped up to the plate. . . . I delegate a lot. . . . I started off being every-where all the time and then as you build up capacity, leadership, you don't have to be everywhere all the time. . . . so I delegate a lot of responsibility to different people . . . assigning myself to the hard-core difficult issues that are controversial, that are going to cause tension either with students or staff, with parents.

This strategy of prioritizing took diverse forms. The principals purposefully learned to delegate and to trust other staff. They figured out what work could wait and what needed to be accomplished immediately, so they could keep their jobs, as well as "sleep at night." Principal Meg summarized the essence of this strat-egy: "Over and over I had to evaluate what is possible now, what can wait, what can I give to someone else, and what do I personally need to do to not go crazy."

Engage in Professional Learning

The sixth professional strategy these principals employed was engaging in pro-fessional learning. Four principals discussed using this strategy to overcome bar-riers to their justice work. "I like to read, I like to learn about what people are doing to make things right," said Principal Natalie. She and Principals Meg, Dale, and Taylor all shared the priority of learning. Their ongoing learning helped them better accomplish their agendas in the face of significant barriers. Their profes-sional learning focused on the needs of their school and areas where they felt their knowledge was more limited. Principal Natalie commented, "The book study groups, the learning we do as a staff, really helped me with some of the stress I feel as far as, am I competent to do this?"

They concentrated on learning about race, language acquisition, disabilities, poverty, curriculum, collaborative teaming structures, cultural practices, build-ing community, math and the current research on mathematical thinking, and developing professional learning communities. Their willingness to learn and their ability to use new knowledge gave them a deeper understanding of their work. Principal Meg articulated the importance of this type of learning: "I learned that some of the ways we're doing inclusive practices isn't working. So, now what can I do to change? I'm learning what we need to do to get there—what strategies or what professional development we need." These principals looked at learning as both a key to gaining new knowledge and skills and as a means to accomplish their social justice agenda.

Build Relationships

The seventh professional strategy these social justice leaders used to sustain and advance their agenda in the face of barriers was building relationships. All seven principals identified building relationships not only as an essential component to their leadership style, but also as a means to overcome the countervailing pressures they faced daily. Principal Tracy explained how important he felt relationships were at his elementary school:

> I spent a lot of time building relationships with families and students and staff. I became incredibly purposeful about it. I think in a way that really helped ease the struggle. . . . It becomes much easier to work with challenging kids if you've built a relationship. . . . when I have to call a parent about an attendance issue and we have a good relationship, even though I'm very serious about it, we can have a productive conversation. I understood them and they trusted me. . . . Even staff who might disagree with a particular idea or initiative felt, "I don't like the idea, but I know [Tracy] cares so much about our kids, I can accept this because I trust him, I know he is being sincere." . . . It also makes the day much more fun; it makes the job more enjoyable. You feel like a part of a community. At first I thought [building relationships] was my job, but it also became very helpful in terms of my emotional well-being.

Principal Scott outlined the efforts he made in building relationships with middle school staff of color. He related a story that demonstrated the nature and power of strong relationships in advancing his agenda:

> One of the African American staff members, she asked me, "Can I ask you a personal question?"
> I said, "Sure."
> "Is your wife Black?"
> "No."
> "Is anybody in your family Black?"
> I said, "Well, yes . . ."

She said, "You have a lot more soul than most White guys."

I took that as a compliment, and then a couple weeks later her good buddy [also African American] transferred to my school, so, I mean, I look at it as there's a certain level of trust.

All seven principals developed relationships with students, staff, and families. They saw these relationships as instrumental to making the changes they felt necessary at their schools. Whether it was relationships with students that made for easier and more effective school discipline, or appreciating and knowing staff and families that created a feeling of mutual respect that allowed for meaningful conversation and trust, these principals used the strategy of building relationships to further social justice in light of the pressures they experienced.

The principals developed and employed seven professional strategies to advance and sustain social justice in the face of significant barriers and resistance, thereby creating time, emotional space, and necessary support to continue their equity and justice work. While their professional strategies enabled these leaders to meet some of the challenges associated with social justice work, the principals did not believe that the strategies made their work easy. They also did not believe that the strategies were enough to sustain their quest for social justice. To accomplish that, they were careful to use personal coping strategies for their lives outside school.

PERSONAL STRATEGIES

Personal strategies were mechanisms that allowed the principals to maintain their equilibrium, so they could continue their efforts in enacting justice. These strategies were distinct from the professional ones in that they were not about rethinking the daily work, but were about staying the course physically and emotionally. The leaders identified six personal coping strategies: prioritize life outside school, use mindful diversions, accept outside validation, engage in regular physical activity, provide for others, and employ potentially harmful behaviors.

Prioritize Life Outside School

The first personal strategy these principals identified to sustain social justice while facing significant pressure involved prioritizing their lives outside of school. While they worked exceedingly long hours, they purposefully set aside time to leave their work and schools behind.

Principal Meg discussed this strategy. It was important for her to keep "feeding myself with friendships, the same kind of people who care about the same thing." She turned to the topic of her family:

I'm purposeful about not cutting time out of my own kids' time. I keep the job between when I, whenever I leave in the morning, whether that's 5:30 or 7:15 a.m. The job ends for me at the latest at 5:00 in the evening and I don't think I've violated that at all, with the exception of night meetings. Very seldom is there any exception to that, in terms of crowding out my own kids' time.

Principal Tracy had a similar outlook:

I was purposeful about making social plans, even if it was just with one person, you know, going out and having a drink, going out and having dinner. That was really helpful. I tried to do that almost weekly. . . . My first year I wasn't really capable of doing that, but I saw the dentist and the doctor a lot that year because, you know what, it made me leave school. . . . A couple of days a week I would pick [my son] up from day care, and I was never late for that. That was our time together and I would make sure I'd leave early on those days. That was great for our relationship and a good strategy.

All seven principals consciously drew the line about when they physically stopped working. While the lines they drew and the time they carved out differed, they agreed that drawing boundaries to make time for their outside life allowed them to maintain essential connections to people who were important to them; further, it helped keep the pressures and huge responsibilities of the job at bay.

Use Mindful Diversions

The second personal strategy the principals developed was using mindful diversions. All seven principals discussed taking part in activities for their own enjoyment for the purpose of getting away from the pressures of work. The diversions cleared their minds of at least some of the stress and turmoil they carried with them from school.

Principal Tracy described the diversions that helped him:

Probably the thing that most helped me with *saving my sanity*, which at times was hanging on by a thread, was Harry Potter. I have read those books so many times. For some reason, I can get so lost in Harry Potter that my mind finally rests.

Principal Natalie discussed activities that she purposefully engaged in for her own enjoyment and that also took her mind off school:

Purposefully, every weekend there's something planned; there's a family thing, a friend thing; there's different groups of people in our lives [and] we try to make sure we get something planned monthly with . . . because you know they're important. We go on trips together; a bunch of us go on trips together and we are stupid and silly.

All these principals acted in purposeful ways outside school, ways that aided them in accomplishing and sustaining their work. The diversions added a certain level of enjoyment to their lives and gave them an opportunity to free themselves from the difficulties of their jobs. All seven principals identified these diversions as necessary strategies to furthering their equity work.

Accept Outside Validation

The third personal strategy used by the principals to sustain their work involved accepting outside validation. They noted that hearing and "taking to heart" the validation they received about their work made a difference in enabling them to continue pursuing social justice. Principal Dale stated:

I think I derive some satisfaction from peers that you respect recognizing your work, who view you as a person who they could learn from; they're willing to ask questions but still to value your opinion. I think that that's a rewarding aspect of the job and sort of sustains you at the same time.

Principal Dale also cited his award from the state Department of Education as a pleasing and also crucial reminder of the importance of his work. As he talked about his award, I noticed a real sense of pride in Principal Dale. While he was humble about it, he gave the impression that receiving this recognition was a source of satisfaction and validated the tough decisions and hard work he had done at his school.

Principal Tracy felt that receiving positive feedback from colleagues, staff, and families enabled him to continue doing his social justice work:

I do not know if I did not receive much or any praise or thanks for my work when I started as a principal or that I just did not let it seep in . . . but [after a few months] hearing and keeping that praise made a difference in sustaining me to do my job. Some days a little reassurance helped a lot.

The principals found strength in hearing and taking to heart the positive praise and validation they received from colleagues, families, students, the community, and national organizations. Principal Eli summarized the underlying sentiment about why this strategy helped sustain and advance their social justice work: "I'm like anybody else, I need to feel like I'm not a total f-up." Big and small recognition helped these principals feel like their work made a difference and that they should push ahead.

Engage in Regular Physical Activity

The fourth personal strategy the seven principals used was engaging in regular physical activity. It helped them keep their bodies in shape to endure the hectic pace of the job and overcome the immense pressure they faced. Principal Eli remarked:

> I exercise. I think physical exercise is really important. . . . You've got to find time to exercise; the best time for me is 5:00 in the morning, so almost every day I get up early. . . . The running is great. I've got a group of people I run with.

Principal Scott, Principal Meg, Principal Taylor, and Principal Tracy all discussed their weekly commitment to exercise as an important self-care strategy. The principals felt this regular and ongoing physical activity helped further their ability to do their work both physically and mentally.

Provide for Others

The fifth personal strategy the principals used was to provide for others. The combination of achieving something tangible and the reward of helping someone made this strategy work for them. Principal Natalie explained:

> I take care of my two uncles and [my neighbor]. . . . We mow lawns for them; we make sure that they have what they need, like dinner and groceries. . . . Those things make me feel like I've done something. . . . Also, probably twice a week I get out and clean up the road for three miles. Things like that are tangible. . . . I can do this; I can mow your lawn and I can help you pack, I can make you a cake, I can do stuff that makes you feel better and makes me feel better in return.

Principal Tracy offered another example:

> We had friends who had a fire in their house, so every week we had them over and fed their entire family. I love to cook, but also I felt every week I was doing something tangible to help someone else. I was feeding people, and I was brought up with the ethnic value about the importance of feeding people, so this felt like I was doing something important. . . .

These dinners may have been good for our friends but making them was
also healing for me.

The principals engaged in service to others as a way of contributing to their
community, but, in return, their service helped them personally and professionally. They experienced a real sense of accomplishment and felt a release from the
pressures of their job. This strategy, while demanding additional time, contributed to maintaining sanity and well-being.

Employ Potentially Harmful Behaviors

The sixth strategy the principals employed to sustain their social justice work while
facing tremendous barriers was to enact potentially harmful behaviors. Five of
the seven principals revealed strategies that were potentially harmful to them. It
is not my intent to judge the principals, but I feel an obligation to report these
strategies, which may have brought some immediate relief, but could have dangerous long-term effects. The two strategies that these principals reported that were
potentially harmful included working harder and drinking alcohol. I will not refer
to the principals here by their pseudonyms in this section, to further protect their
anonymity.

Five of the principals noted that one of their strategies included "working
harder" when faced with barriers. One principal said, "That would mean me putting in more early morning time or night time, taking away from the personal time,
so I don't let the kid down. . . . It just means you're going to work harder." In
discussing how a particular principal dealt with the overwhelming demands of
the job, this principal replied, "I work more hours." This principal stressed that
the normal workweek consisted of 65 to 80 hours. In that case, working more hours
meant an even longer week, of upward of 90 hours. Another principal said:

> I felt I always wanted to get more done. I tried to outwork the job. I would
> do more and more things, work harder, work longer. . . . My best tools
> coming into this position were that I could outwork and outthink just
> about anyone or any problem.

In addition to adding more work on top of an already demanding position,
three of the principals discussed using alcohol as a strategy. One principal drank
alcohol as a way to feel alive and to cope with pressure and resistance: "I was
definitely drinking more and more. I needed to be able to get away from the enormity of this work. I needed to feel happier again." Another said, "I probably do a
lot more drinking so I can be more social because there's a lot emotionally that
builds up with this work and you want to feel OK and I want to make everybody's
life OK . . . and that's a stress." While these principals were aware of the poten-

tial dangers, they used alcohol at least in part as a strategy to relax in order to continue to advance social justice.

In sum, the seven principals developed and used both personal and professional strategies to advance social justice in the face of resistance. They attributed their success in making their schools more equitable at least in part to the strategies they developed. Some of the strategies helped the principals accomplish more for the most marginalized students and make the school a better place. Other strategies helped "ease the pain" or allowed them "to sleep at night." They believed that by using a combination of strategies, they were able to make and better sustain social justice as a part of their schools.

CONCLUSION

In looking across the professional and personal strategies discussed here, a key lesson is the importance of bringing people together to sustain this work. One way to look at this is that these principals in various ways organized groups around them to further their agenda and sustain their commitment to social justice. They found other leaders to build a supportive administrative network. They brought school staff together to make key decisions and, in doing so, developed a shared sense of commitment and responsibility. They developed relationships with many stakeholders that helped further their work and sustain them. These leaders relied on and purposefully maintained social and family networks outside school that provided emotional support and gave them additional ways to feel valued. An important implication for practicing principals is that seeking out and establishing connections with other school leaders who hold similar beliefs about equity and justice is beneficial. Finding, communicating with, and supporting other leaders who are engaged in social justice action nourishes principals by providing support and reassurance, exposing them to varied perspectives grounded in equity, easing the isolation of the position, and giving them an opportunity to help others. Creating supportive structures in school, building relationships with school staff and families, and maintaining social and family networks are integral aspects of effective leadership.

The principals believed that an essential feature of maintaining a commitment to equity and justice was understanding and being comfortable with themselves, their strengths, and their limitations. Along with this understanding of self, an important lesson about fostering resilience is creating a place for the discussion, development, and teaching of strategies to advance justice in the face of resistance.

To be clear, the strategies the principals reported do not represent a checklist for current and future social justice leaders to complete so they may counter the resistance they face. While certain ideas that the leaders related may resonate with particular administrators' needs and lives, there is a real danger in viewing their strategies as a finite list of tasks to complete. While the principals felt that their strategies helped them deal with the resistance they faced, they did not characterize them as a cure. It was a messy and ongoing process. Still, the strategies do act as entry points into how to maintain sanity while furthering justice work. Discussing these strategies both allows leaders to learn new ways to protect their well-being and fulfill their duties and opens an important conversation about the vulnerable and evolutionary nature of leadership.

Working on personal and professional self-care was part of what helped these principals find relief from the resistance they faced. It was not that they exercised and then felt better about their work, or found a network of supportive colleagues and were suddenly able to restructure their school, or drank alcohol and could as a result cope with the intense anger they experienced. As noted earlier, it was an untidy and continuing struggle. It was a process of learning to approach their jobs sometimes in slightly and other times in radically different ways. It was a process of the principals' learning how to protect and maintain their lives outside their schools.

Without mechanisms of self-care, leaders capable of creating more just and equitable schools can burn out. This can lead to the principal's either leaving the position that so desperately needs him or her or slowly but steadily accepting a compromised vision of equity. Both these options are equally bleak. Social justice leadership is dependent not only on a belief in and vision of equity and the capacity to initiate equity-oriented changes, but also on the ability to sustain such work and nourish oneself in the process.

CHAPTER 9

"The Intricacies and Details":
Consciousness, Knowledge, Skills,
and Core Traits of Social Justice Leaders

No problem can be solved by the same consciousness that created it.
We need to see the world anew.

—Albert Einstein

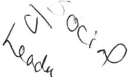

A PPLYING EINSTEIN'S words to the educational leadership context suggests that traditional traits and consciousness have been inadequate for SJL. This chapter returns to the social justice leader, using leaders' work, words, and experiences to highlight the two keys to SJL positioned at the center of the framework. It is important to note that the discussion of SJL begins with and then comes back again to the actual leader, with a discussion of the first and second keys to SJL from Chapter 1:

Key 1. Acquire a broad, reconceptualizd consciousness/knowledge/skills base.
Key 2. Possess core leadership traits.

This chapter begins with a discussion of the consciousness, knowledge, and skills the principals relied on in their work to increase access, improve teaching and curriculum, and create a climate of belonging. Their core leadership traits evolved from these knowledges, skills, and dispositions; thus the discussion of these traits will come second.

ACQUIRING BROAD, RECONCEPTUALIZED
CONSCIOUSNESS, KNOWLEDGE, AND SKILLS

This key to SJL is framed around specific ways these principals sought to enact social justice in their schools. Three distinct examples of how they improved their

schools with regard to equity and justice were common across all seven principals, and they highlight the social justice consciousness, knowledge, and skills
these leaders relied on to make these reforms at their schools. This section will
include a brief description of the specific ways the principals advanced social
justice, a discussion of the social justice consciousness they possessed that aided
them in their work, and a discussion of the knowledge and skills they possessed
to help make that advancement successful. I will discuss knowledge and skills
together, as there was significant overlap between possessing knowledge, and the
ability to use it effectively, and skills. I will highlight one strategy they used from
each of the ways they sought to change injustice in Chapters 3, 4, and 5 to highlight the consciousness, knowledge, and skills that provide lessons for leadership
preparation: 1) eliminate pullout and separate programs, 2) provide ongoing staff
development focused on building equity, and 3) reach out to marginalized families and the community.

Eliminate Pullout and Segregated Programs

All seven principals created and maintained inclusive services for students with
varying academic and social needs. In their words, they enacted justice by "eliminating pullout and segregated special ed, ESL, Title I, and talented and gifted
programs," and replacing them with "inclusive services for every child." They
also enacted social justice in this manner by "eliminating tracking in math." They
moved their schools to a heterogeneously taught inquiry-based mathematics curriculum. In their efforts to eliminate pullout and separate programs they relied on
particular aspects of a social justice consciousness and particular knowledge and
skills. These efforts were discussed in detail in Chapter 3.

Social Justice Consciousness. One of the most critical elements to their
social justice consciousness that the principals described as vital to their ability to
develop inclusive school norms was a "bold vision." One principal described this:

> Ultimately our restructuring [to eliminate pullout and segregated pro-
> grams] was about seeing a "better way." I could see beyond the status quo
> that was present in my school, and in many schools, that sorts and labels
> kids. . . . Getting past that status quo was about a belief in and a vision of
> inclusive norms where all students are challenged and have access to the
> good stuff—quality teaching and serious curriculum.

Not only did this principal and her counterparts "see a better way," but they
held fast to a belief that inclusive services and heterogeneous grouping benefited
all students. Another principal discussed this: "Creating inclusive special education services and detracking math made our middle school better not only for our

struggling students but for every child. They all could and did benefit from multiple adults working in their classrooms and a rigorous and inquiry based math curriculum. I have always believed this, and our achievement after these changes has confirmed this." Within these principals' belief in inclusive services is a belief in what one principal called "differentiation and teaming." He went on:

> Teachers can differentiate their curriculum and instruction to meet a wide range of needs and if they don't know how, they can learn. . . . Plus, one of the best ways to meet that range is through team-teaching. Multiple adults [general education teachers, special education teachers, ESL teachers, assistants, and reading teachers] working together within the classroom to plan and teach the range of students does work. They have to work together in sometimes new and different ways, but the whole is greater than the sum of its parts. *Plan when?*

The seven principals also embodied a consciousness that a sense of belonging and classroom community are imperative to learning. One principal said, "When we keep pulling kids out of their classrooms we create marginalized community members." Another principal stated, "Students' connections to their peers and to their teacher are essential, but all the pullout programs and tracking that was going on really undermine those essential aspects of school." He continued, "We know what happens when you feel connected to something and to people; your motivation goes up, you work harder, you are a better person. Creating truly inclusive classrooms and schools takes advantage of our need to feel important and connected."

Their bold vision, belief that inclusive schools benefit all students, commitment to differentiation and teaming, belief that a sense of belonging and a sense of community are disrupted by pullout and segregated programs, and sense of assured humility together constructed a social justice consciousness. The principals relied upon this consciousness to enact this particular aspect of social justice leadership. Additionally, they possessed and used certain knowledge and skills to eliminate pullout and segregated programs.

Relevant Knowledge and Skills. The principals could not rely on their social justice consciousness alone to eliminate pullout and segregated programs. They possessed and required various knowledge and skills to enact this form of social justice. Building upon their belief that inclusive services were better for all students, the leaders possessed at least some knowledge of research on inclusion, tracking, and heterogeneous grouping. None of the principals would argue that they had "expert" knowledge or could "cite numerous authors" in these areas but they possessed enough of this knowledge base that they felt they understood. One principal said, "The university types could cite all the research on inclusion, but I have retained enough that I know there is a body of research that says students with and without disabilities have academic and social gains in inclusive settings." Another stated, "I know enough research on tracking and grouping to understand that tracking sentences low tracked kids to dead end futures, and that heterogeneous groups, when done right, benefit everybody."

Along with their knowledge about inclusion and tracking, these principals had or gained a working knowledge of special education and services for English-language learners (ELLs). Four of the principals talked specifically about having little knowledge about ELLs and enrolled in university courses or participated in administrator study groups to bolster their knowledge base in this area. One principal described his use of special education and ELL knowledge and skills:

> If I did not understand enough about special ed and ESL, then I would have to rely solely on others and on the way things have always been done. The fact that I know what works and what doesn't, and I know enough about disability and special ed law and language acquisition and non-native English speakers, means I am ahead of the game; I can use that to create service delivery models, I can use that when I am speaking with teachers and families.

Another principal continued this line of thinking:

> If I did not know that pullout ESL programs are the least effective, then I probably would not have worked so hard to change ours.

Additionally, these principals knew how to work with and understand their school's data and possessed the skills to use that data with their staff and community members. It was a combination of data and presentation skills that aided in their efforts to lead for social justice. One principal noted:

> I started collecting data on where our students went for special programs (special ed, ESL, Title I, talented and gifted) and who went to each, who did not leave the classroom, and who left more than once. I started seeing disturbing patterns in regards to race and income. With this data I could paint an accurate picture to share with my staff and families. It was this picture—that pretty much only the middle-class White kids remained in the class—that really drove home to others our need for change.

Another principal commented,

> Once I got a handle on our data, I could use it effectively with staff and families. I mean, who can continue to argue that things are "good enough" when only 30% of our Black kids are reading on grade level, that only

> 13% of our kids in special education are meeting our standards. . . . That data helped make the case for inclusive services . . . but it also was in the way I had to say it to my teachers. I needed a great amount of finesse, because they hear from lots of people, "Schools suck," and "You're not doing your job," so I had to constantly frame my use of data in ways that were not about blaming our teachers but seeing that we can have more success doing things differently.

The principals had a handle on how to collect and use data, but it was their use of the school data that is perhaps more important. They knew how to present it to multiple audiences and they approached data with their own equity lens.

These principals also possessed knowledge and skills in diverse content areas. One high school principal explained, "I needed to have a basic working knowledge of high school science in order to articulate how I could see inclusive science working." Another principal remarked, "I am not a math teacher by trade, but by understanding the direction that mathematics is headed and understanding some about inquiry based math, I could play the role I needed in moving our school to detrack math." Another principal said, "My knowledge of early literacy was instrumental in helping people understand how inclusive services for ESL students and struggling readers could really happen and happen well." Their understanding of content areas and strong instructional practices were vital knowledge and skills they relied on as they improved their schools.

These principals possessed the knowledge and skills to be effective instructional leaders; however, they also needed management skills to make their vision of eliminating pullout and segregated programs a reality. One principal asserted,

> It was not enough that I could believe [inclusive restructuring] was possible, I needed to be able to put the structures in place to make it happen. . . . I expected that my teachers would team-teach and team-plan, so I had to create teams of adults who could work together effectively. I had to create a schedule that would support that teaming relationship. . . . I needed to create class placement procedures that would create inclusive and balanced classrooms that did not overload any one class. . . . It was the combination of knowing it was possible with making it possible that made our inclusive services work.

While the leaders possessed both depth and breath in their knowledge base, they clearly needed management skills to make their schools run under the new systems they helped create. They saw the deep connections between their managerial skills and their vision of more socially just schools.

These social justice principals possessed knowledge and skills regarding inclusive services benefiting all students, special education, ELL, understanding and presenting data, content and curriculum, and management skills to make their vision a reality. This range of knowledge and skills supported their social justice consciousness to eliminate pullout and segregated programs.

② Provide Ongoing Staff Development Focused on Building Equity

The principals' efforts to create more socially just schools took numerous forms. I turn now to how these principals provided ongoing staff development focused on building equity. As the principals identified issues where there was discrepant achievement they facilitated continuing learning around those topics. This staff development addressed issues from literacy to math, from collaboration to ELL. All seven school leaders also fostered formal and informal learning and conversations about race. These efforts were described in Chapter 4. In what follows, the principals' social justice consciousness and knowledge and skills are framed by examining their efforts to provide staff development focused on equity gaps.

   Social Justice Consciousness. Their efforts to provide ongoing staff development focused on equity gaps was grounded in a belief that "teachers are professionals." The principals were firm in their belief that their teachers were capable people and deserved professional respect. One principal stated, "The teachers I work with are trained professionals and need to be treated accordingly." Another principal said, "I believe I should act in a manner that conveys respect for the teaching profession." He continued:

> To that end, I can expect that professionals will continue to learn and expand their abilities. . . . I can also expect that they are capable of teaching all students. This is a statement of serious respect. I believe we do not need "teacher proof" curriculum or scripted programs. We have professionals who may and in fact do require new learning, but who ultimately, with greater understanding and abilities, are capable of teaching and reaching each and every child.

This principal felt it was the responsibility of educators to undertake ongoing learning. In addition, it was their beliefs about, confidence in, and support of their teachers that positioned teachers not as incompetent or needing "teacher proof" solutions but as trained professionals capable of learning and ultimately of enacting an equity agenda. It was this sincere belief that grounded the seven principals as they sought to provide significant and ongoing professional development.

   Along with seeing teachers as professionals who could and should undergo continual learning, the principals possessed a commitment to their own learning. As stated previously, four of the principals did not have a sufficient knowledge base around ELL issues and were committed to learning more. All seven felt the impact of their own learning on their ability to be social justice leaders.

One principal put it thus: "How can I be an effective supervisor in the area of math unless I understand math and the current thinking about teaching math? So I went to this 2-week summer course on supervising math and inquiry-based math, and I have committed to a math study group." Another principal said, "If I am expecting my staff to better understand English language learners, I better learn alongside them." They were committed to their own growth and development and they saw it as their duty to model this but also as a necessity around areas of equity gaps. They were reflective enough to realize where they needed to enhance their own learning as a part of identifying the equity gaps for their school.

In providing ongoing staff development, along with their respect for teachers as professionals and a commitment to their own learning, these principals maintained a belief that rejected deficit thinking (Valencia, 1997) and embraced, valued, and understood the diversity of their schools and communities. A principal explained, "Race matters and having the ability to confront and discuss issues of race and racism are paramount to why our staff needed to engage in learning and discussing race." Another principal stated,

> If I accepted the notion that Black and Brown students couldn't achieve or that poor kids would never measure up, or the students with disabilities were not capable of serious academics, then I would not have bothered to create a better school or bothered to have my teachers learn better ways of teaching reading. But I do not believe that. . . . So we have to learn more; we have to learn best practice in literacy, in collaboration; we have to discuss race and equity. Our learning matters a great deal. Our learning contains a quiet respect to our students that says, "We may not know everything but we will not let you fail."

This "quiet respect" echoed through how the principals approached staff development at their schools. They purposefully brought issues of race and diversity into discussions and professional learning opportunities because they felt the need to work against notions of deficit thinking and to try to ground their schools in a valuing of diversity.

The principals possessed a belief in their teachers as professionals, a commitment to their own learning, and an understanding and valuing of diversity. These elements of their social justice consciousness helped them in their work to provide ongoing professional development focused on equity gaps. Along with this consciousness, they possessed knowledge and skills in this area.

Relevant Knowledge and Skills. A key aspect of their knowledge and skills in leading this ongoing professional development was their understanding of

curriculum and instruction. For example, one principal facilitated professional
learning for her staff in the area of mathematics:

> I recognized that one key issue in regards to equity in my school was the
> way math was taught. I know enough about math to realize hey, we are
> not all teaching math the way it should be taught. . . . Without that
> knowledge I would be allowed to think, "Everything is fine," or think,
> "We are teaching math and our students aren't becoming deep math
> thinkers, so what is wrong with our kids?" Both of those conclusion would
> have been very harmful to our students . . . To me it makes the case for
> why principals need breadth of curricular knowledge.

The principal quoted above provided a clear example of the power of particular
knowledge in content areas that helped lead professional development focused
on identified equity gaps. The principals' own content knowledge was a key part
of their social justice leadership.

While these principals possessed knowledge and skills in curriculum and
instruction, they also knew how and when to access other resources. The principal who spoke of primary literacy clearly relied and knew when to rely on a reading coach for his teachers. Additionally, another principal shared, "We needed to
do a lot of learning around teaching students who are non-native English speakers." She continued,

> I connected with a new professor at [the local university] whose area was
> ESL, and we arranged for her to teach university courses at our school.
> That allowed for almost every single member of my staff, teachers,
> assistants, the secretary, the custodian, the art teacher, the PE teacher, and
> me to take classes in teaching ESL.

The combination of having sufficient knowledge in content and instruction
and making connections to effectively utilized capable outside resources was an
essential piece in providing ongoing staff development focused on equity gaps.
The principals knew content area curriculum and instruction, yet they actively
rejected the incestuous notion that people from outside organizations had nothing to offer their schools or could not understand the realities of their students.

Moreover, all seven principals led formal and informal learning about issues
of race. They felt they needed a level of comfort and sufficient thinking about
race to facilitate these conversations. One principal captured what each principal
had noted:

> I have done significant reading, thinking, discussing, and arguing about
> race. That has not given me a sense of enlightenment about racial issues,

but a comfort with having language to discuss race. Having that comfort and language were key to my abilities to confront racial issues and essential to my ability to help my staff wrestle with issues about race.

None of the principals would consider her- or himself an "expert" on racial issues, but they all were comfortable freely discussing issues of race. As mentioned, six of the principals were White, and these White principals saw their White administrator colleagues and many of their White teachers as "extremely uncomfortable" in discussing and examining racial issues. It was their ability to engage in and speak about issues of race that they felt was a key aspect in helping their staff members engage in and learn about racial issues.

In tackling issues of race and creating a more just school, the principals relied on their ability to see the interconnected nature of equity throughout their schools. This was one of the reasons each of the principals led discussions about race. A principal commented:

> Our achievement is about how we teach math, it is about how and what we teach in social studies, but it is also about how we understand race and disability and class. It is about how we see our students and we have a lot of baggage at my school in terms of seeing our students of color, students with disabilities, and poor students in an equitable light. We can improve our math curriculum and instruction but it will never be enough unless we deal with our attitudes and beliefs about race, disability, and poverty.

Seeing the interconnected nature of issues at school is a key skill that the leaders possessed as they enacted social justice in their schools. It was seeing the interconnected nature of issues that helped the leaders move beyond traditional school improvement efforts. While many leaders develop content knowledge and skills, and many bring in outside resources and experts to support professional development, and a growing number of districts are touching on racial issues, it was the leaders' ability to connect all these that was a vital aspect of their knowledge and skills. The interconnected nature of issues helped guide the kinds of professional development they planned for their school staffs.

Finally, these principals again required particular management knowledge and skills to provide the ongoing professional learning. They needed to be able to work within the negotiated contracts for teachers and staff to find appropriate ways to provide training and learning. They needed to know and understand how to use release time, substitute teachers, and budget monies to pay staff for time outside the contract day. One principal explained what this meant:

> I know understanding the teacher contract is not a glamorous part of my job, but without that I would have violated the contract when we were

arranging professional development opportunities. I am a firm believer that if you want people to learn new things and get out of their comfort zone, you cannot exploit their time. . . . The two professional development days built into the calendar are not nearly enough, so I have to use sub days and create time for meetings and mentoring and modeling right within the school day. If I violated the contract, then people would not have to participate or would resent participating, and either of those get us nowhere.

The principals possessed an understanding of curriculum and instruction across content areas, obtained access to talented outside resources, had language and experience in confronting issues of race, understood the interconnected nature of equity, and had the necessary management skills to make professional learning happen. This complex combination of knowledge and skills helped the principals enact social justice in their schools.

Reach Out to Marginalized Families and Community

The final example used to frame social justice principals' consciousness, knowledge, and skills is how they reached out to marginalized families and community. This is discussed in detail in Chapter 5. The principals made concerted efforts to connect to families who traditionally had not been active in their school and to make bridges with the community. This included "facilitating monthly ethnic parents meetings," "making home visits every week," "making purposeful positive contact with families of color, families who struggle financially, and families who are non-native English speakers," "building relationships with community organizations and social services agencies," and "working with the city, police, housing, and public health officials to create a neighborhood resource center." The principals possessed distinct consciousness as well as knowledge and skills to enact this form of social justice.

Social Justice Consciousness. The principals saw beyond traditional ways in which schools, families, and community related. They could imagine multiple ways to connect the school with its neighborhood and families. One of the principals described such a vision:

When I arrived at my school, pretty much only the middle-class White families were officially involved with the school and I heard over and over, "We try and we try but we can't get other families involved in the Parent Teacher Organization." That, right there, was part of the problem; we needed to see other possibilities beyond the PTO—to reach out to our families in multiple ways. . . . All people were talking about was the PTO, but there was no thought of all the other ways we could develop deep meaningful relationships between our school and our families.

The principals had a vision to build relationships and to be present in all parts of their school neighborhoods. This included inviting diverse and traditionally nonactive families, in particular, to be involved in different ways and, in doing so, they developed personal connections with these families. They believed that they needed to connect and have systematic communication with non-English-speaking families in purposeful and consistent ways.

While the specific visions of the multiple ways to connect with families and the community varied principal by principal, they all possessed a belief and vision that looked beyond the traditional and present ways their schools had connected with families and communities. In facing an historic disconnect between their schools and marginalized families, they rejected the prevailing sentiment they encountered that "nothing could be done." They believed, as one principal put it, that "just because it hadn't been done at this school, does not mean that I was not going to connect with my Black, Spanish-speaking, Hmong-speaking, and low-income families. It can and in fact did happen." Along with that vision, the principals possessed a deep consciousness of valuing diversity. That same principal continued:

> I needed to connect with my Hmong community. The Hmong community wanted to meet together with school officials monthly, so we made that happen. We needed to hear each other. I could see that the school had not deeply connected with the Hmong families before, that their kids were accepted but not "loved," that their struggles were tolerated but not embraced, that the Hmong community was seen as "here to stay" but not part of the fabric of our school. They were kept on the margins of the school agenda and the margins of many staff members' hearts. This needed to change and it did.

This principal's consciousness provides a challenge to diverse schools everywhere. She sees the continued marginalization of particular groups of students and families when diversity is accepted but not deeply valued. Her embracing of the diversity present in her school positions students historically and currently in the "margins" in a manner that allows her school to move to a more just place.

Within these principals' vision for interacting with families and their commitment to valuing diversity, they possessed a belief in a holistic approach to working with youth and families. They believed in what one principal called "the big picture" or the "long haul." She continued:

> We can put Band-Aids on their problems and use punitive and reactionary strategies to conflict and behavior, but in reality their issues are too

complex to Band-Aid. Or we have a choice; we can commit to the long
haul with our kids and listen and talk with them, give them second
chances, and reach out to their families and communities.

This principal described her belief in seeing students and families in complex and holistic ways. All seven believed that the young people they worked with
were complicated, important, and deserving of much more than short-term reac-
tions to their issues and lives.

In addition, the principals had a drive to connect their schools with the community. One principal said, "We cannot operate in a vacuum. Our kids go back
and forth between us and their neighborhood, and we need to show them the connections: academic connections, emotional connection, and social connections.
. . . We need to work with multiple groups and agencies. We have to work in the
community." The principals believed it was their responsibility, and that it was
essential, to connect with people and agencies beyond the school walls.

The social justice principals possessed a vision to see multiple ways of interacting with families and community, a deep valuing of the diversity in their schools,
a belief in a holistic approach to working with students and families, and a commitment to engaging with the community. All these were important components
of their social justice consciousness. Additionally, as they reached out to marginalized families and community they relied on a set of knowledge and skills.

Relevant Knowledge and Skills. A pivotal knowledge and skill these principals possessed in this work was an understanding of the importance of relationships and the ability to develop them with diverse families and community
members. One principal stated, "I may not be Mr. Charisma, but I certainly know
how to connect with the range of our families." Another principal said,

> Let me give you an example: I had the best postsuspension conference
> with an African American mom who was mad as hell at me for suspending
> her daughter. But the reason I say it was the best conference was that we
> really could talk about what had happened. . . . We could have a real
> discussion; we could argue and in the end we could really hear each other.
> And that only happened because we had a relationship.

The principals understood the need to build relationships person by person
and could do so. In seeing one of the principals at a family open house, I clearly
saw these relationships in action. I saw a sea of students and their families, all
different skin colors, speaking a variety of languages, and everybody interacting
with positive energy with the principal. He tried phrases in Spanish and Hmong—
not with any fluency, but the effort was there. I took away from this experience

that this principal had developed relationships with very many families. It was clear to me that he cared deeply about them and that they reciprocated his warmth.

These principals relied on interpersonal communication skills as they built their relationships. One principal explained, "I spend a concerted amount of time making sure I communicate with all families. It is a priority to make sure there is an open flow of information. This means listening carefully as well as clearly written or clearly spoken communication."

Their skills in communicating were important in reaching out to families and community members. They also possessed particular management skills in order to be successful in this endeavor. They knew how to organize people to rally around important issues; they knew how to make sure there was transportation and child care available for families for evening school events. The principals scheduled time for community outreach and home visits. The management of the issues necessary for ongoing involvement with diverse families was integral to the principals' ability to maintain strong relationships with traditionally marginalized families.

They felt these skills were not "flashy" and not the "most glamorous part of the job," but were vital in their abilities to connect with families and community. The principals attributed their management skills, along with their interpersonal communication and ability to develop relationships, as essential in allowing them to successfully reach out to marginalized families and communities. Their knowledge and skills combined with the consciousness described above enabled these leaders to enact this form of social justice.

In sum, using three of the strategies the principals used to advance social justice provided a means to highlight both the social justice consciousness as well as the knowledge and skills they possessed. Their consciousness and knowledge and skills were instrumental in their ability to create and maintain more just and equitable schools. Table 9.1 outlines all the features of the social justice consciousness and the knowledge and skills these leaders demonstrated that were highlighted in this chapter.

POSSESSING CORE LEADERSHIP TRAITS

In seeking to understand SJL, it is important to recognize that while what influenced these principals in their becoming social justice leaders differed, as discussed in Chapter 2, out of these paths and their social justice consciousness, knowledge and skills evolved into a number of common leadership qualities. These are discussed next.

Understanding leadership traits is a way to more deeply understand who social justice leaders are and how they work. In describing these common traits, I do not

Table 9.1. Consciousness, knowledge, and skills of social justice principals.

Social Justice Consciousness	Knowledge	Skills
Possesses a bold vision	Research on inclusion, tracking, and heterogeneous grouping	Using and presenting data
Believes that inclusive services and heterogeneous grouping benefit all students	Special education: policy, procedures, disability information, and practice	Interpersonal communication
Is committed to differentiation and teaming	Using and presenting data	Language/experience/comfort with issues of race
Believes a sense of belonging and of classroom community are imperative for learning	English Language Learners: research, policy, and practice	Accessing talented outside resources
Sees teachers as professionals	Content area curriculum and instruction	Developing relationships with diverse people
Is committed to own learning and learning of others	Interconnected nature of equity in schools	Management skills: scheduling, creating service delivery and staffing patterns, facilitating class placement, working within negotiated contracts, utilizing release time, creating resources for professional development, organizing people, arranging transportation and child care, scheduling proactive time for outreach
Understands and values diversity	Race, identity, and privilege	
Believes in holistic approach to working with students and families		
Is committed to engaging with the community		

mean to imply that this is a monolithic group of principals. The leaders came to their position by different routes, but they also differ greatly in leadership style and personality. Some are soft-spoken and reserved, and others gregarious and outgoing. Some have a commanding presence when they enter a group and others are unassuming. Some enjoy the spotlight and are often in front of the entire school, while others organize events to minimize the need for them to take center stage. Some are spontaneous in their daily schedules and others methodical in their use of a detailed calendar. Their offices range from visually tidy to containing piles of paper and materials that are strewn throughout. Some are most passionate about racial issues, others are most passionate about inclusive schooling, and still others do not identify a central guiding issue. Some of these principals arrive hours before school starts and others work late into the evening. In many ways these principals are as different as they are similar.

However, they all possess common leadership traits that are central to their social justice work. They embody a complicated mix of humility and a confidence bordering on arrogance, lead with intense visionary passion, and maintain a tenacious commitment to a vision of social justice while nurturing and empowering their staff. I begin with explaining the sense of what I call arrogant humility. Since, it was the least straightforward trait, more illustrations are provided than with the other two traits whose descriptions follow.

Arrogant Humility

Throughout this project, the principals showed a personal sense of arrogant humility in various ways. I define this as a paradoxical blend of arrogance and humility. The arrogance means that these principals have a headstrong belief that they are right; they know what is best, and they feel they are the ones needed to lead toward that vision. The humility comes from a continual self-doubt of their abilities and knowledge, their willingness to admit mistakes both publicly and privately, and their questioning whether they are doing any good in their positions. This humility echoes Skrla's (2000) explanation about the necessity of school leaders who challenge discrimination possessing a reflective nature.

It is important to note that many researchers with whom I have shared this work feel that this "arrogance" appears to be more accurately described as "intense confidence." However, during a group debriefing with the principals, they preferred the phrase "arrogant humility" to "confident humility," the former resonating authentically with their style and identities. I defer to their preference.

One principal captured this complex nature with statements such as "I am the keeper of the flame. . . . I am the one who has made this happen. I kept it going. I provided the vision and resources. . . . Me, I did it," in combination with "I'm doing all I can, but is it really making a difference? I wonder if I have done any good. I wonder if someone else could do more."

To further understand this arrogant humility, another principal within the same few sentences displayed real confidence and self-importance vis-à-vis this work and at the same time was self-deprecating and unsure. She said, "I know I am right. I run this national organization. . . . I have made a difference; I continue to make a difference. Clearly I am good at what I do or all this [improvements in student achievement and positive changes in curriculum and climate] wouldn't get done and I would not be able to run this school and the national organization" in combination with "I'm very ignorant in some situations. I realize how small my knowledge base is. . . . I don't feel like I've done anything right."

The arrogant side of the seemingly contradictory combination was apparent as Principal Meg shared thoughts on how to improve leadership preparation. "My presenting at leadership classes at the university would make [the preparation program] better. . . . I've been invited to be on this [national commission]. . . . I received this national award. I am as good as it gets. Bring those leadership students on. I could teach future principals a lot and they'd be better for it."

Yet her humility was evident as she discussed times when her actions and changes in the school had perhaps unjust or negative consequences for particular people. Principal Meg reflected upon their schoolwide restructuring:

> Two veteran teachers left the school to work elsewhere when it became clear we were going forward with this [restructuring]. While ultimately the restructuring was more inclusive, the right thing to do, and better for all of our students and in particular our students of color and students learning English, there must have been negative consequences on [the veteran teachers]. . . . Was this *just* for them? It's hard to say yes.

She explained that clearly she believed in the direction she had taken the school, but knew that that these two teachers' lives had been affected and she was certainly reflecting on the injustice and power relationships in those negative consequences for them. Principal Meg provided an example of this complex combination of headstrong, confident leadership wound tightly with a reflective, humble perspective.

Principal Tracy offers another look at arrogant humility. In terms of his arrogance, he said, "Look at our student achievement gains, look at the changes that have happened. It is comprehensive. . . . Achievement gains, structure, climate, community services, family relations, stronger curriculum, and a positive and welcoming atmosphere; you name it, it happened. I did that. I am responsible for this happening. I am damn good. Tell me, who else does all that?"

In understanding the combination of arrogance and humility, I felt it was essential to position this arrogance alongside his reflection on supervision of staff. He remarked:

> One year, I needed to take disciplinary action on a teacher of color. And, while this was the right thing to do for the kids—many of whom were students of color—to advocate for the students involved, their rights, and interests, I have come back to this time and time again. Am I being the oppressor to a teacher of color? We all know their voices have historically been devalued; their actions are misrepresented oftentimes in negative

ways. Just as with students of color, they are disciplined more often for the same thing White counterparts do. Am I enacting injustice? Am I being a tool of oppression? . . . I question myself every day, not only about this, but I wonder, am I the right person to do this? Am I the one this school needs? Some days I feel like I just can't do this job.

In seeing his arrogance next to the kind of reflective troubling of when his actions may have had negative affects, Principal Tracy provides example of this complicated mix of arrogant humility. These leaders offered examples of situations in which they recognized that there was a possibility of injustice being perpetrated by them. It is this ability to reflect and see these possibilities of injustice that contribute significantly to both humility and in turn to the complexity of their leadership. In sum, one principal explained the arrogant humility that this group embodies:

I wear my heart on my sleeve. I am a real person with my staff, families, and students. I know what I think is best and I know what I think needs to happen, but I'm willing to be silly and make fun of myself and also I'm very serious about the kind of school our kids deserve, but I'm always passionate; I laugh and even cry with these people. . . . Yes, I am full of myself, and yes, I make plenty of mistakes, and yes, I admit both freely.

This arrogance, self-confidence, and comfort with themselves, in combination with sincere humility, insecurity, and self-doubt create a very complicated and dynamic leader. The mix of knowing they are right and freely admitting when they are wrong or do not know something conveys to people around them the sense that they are real people. Their willingness, ability, and constant reflection on their actions, mistakes, and decisions set these social justice leaders apart from traditional leaders.

I felt in meeting and getting to know these leaders that this is a group of very intelligent people. Their intelligence adds to their arrogance because they know that they are smart. It also adds to their ability to get things done because they understand the technical aspects of the job, they understand culture, they understand people, they understand special education, they understand curriculum, they have language and skills to talk about race, they understand ELL, they understand scheduling, and they possess the ability and drive to learn and learn quickly. Further, this intelligence cannot be separated from either the successes they achieve toward justice or the discouragement they felt personally as a result of the resistance they faced in their social justice work, discussed in detail in Chapter 7. I have come to believe that this intelligence is truly a double-edged sword. It allows the principals to understand issues and creatively work toward solutions, but at the same time it forces them to see problems, and the weight of those problems bears heavily upon them. They believe it is their responsibility and their calling to fix these problems. A dramatic tension exists because of their intelligence. The cliché "Ignorance is bliss" fits with how these leaders described their work. One principal stated:

> I looked around at other principals and realized that some people just didn't care or understand [special education, social justice, ELL]. . . . They weren't worrying about them; they weren't losing sleep. . . . Sometimes that seemed like an easier and softer way to live. They did not get it, so they did not have to worry about it.

It is not only the intelligence and arrogance that allows success in moving toward justice; it is the humility. This humility brings a willingness to be open and genuine with staff and families. Combining a desire to learn with an attitude that will let the learning become part of their practice, the humility brings self-doubt, which, like intelligence, adds to the struggle and pain. These principals leading for social justice act both confident and uncertain at the same time. They know they are right, yet are unsure if they are doing any good. They make big changes and they question whether they belong in their position. They act larger than life but also come across as down to earth. This core aspect permits them to do remarkable things and delivers certain discouragement. Arrogant humility helps define them and impels in part the passion that drives their work.

Passionate Vision

The social justice principals worked not as bureaucrats, not as middle managers, but as passionate leaders. Operationally, passionate leadership is having a tightly interwoven connection between the principal position and the person doing that job. In their caring so deeply, having such deep commitment, and maintaining such sincere enthusiasm about their work, there is little separation between the leadership and the leaders. They achieved this by holding, maintaining, and championing a strong vision while embodying the qualities that Shields (2004) and Furman and Gruenewald (2004) describe about transformative leadership. This passionate leadership seeks to change people's beliefs and values from self-centered to other centered. Additionally, they complement that effort with working toward the moral purpose of social justice. In explaining his passion for social justice leadership, one principal described the difference between a "good" principal and the social justice leader:

> [Traditional] good leaders are technocrats. They write good memos, they write good reports, they stay out of trouble, and they're OK; they're in OK places but they don't have any passion for anything; they're just techni-

cally very adept but they have no sense of passion or feel or vision. They just go through life and they're proficient in what they do. . . . Principals are like musicians. There are some musicians who play all the right notes, but there's no feel to them. Then there's some people who do everything, they play all the right notes and have a passion. Then there are people who are less technically gifted and the passion compensates.

This principal sees the social justice leader in both the last two descriptions, but attributed the big difference in their work to their passion. This work connects closely with who these principals are as people. They see themselves as tightly interwoven with their positions. One principal stated, "This is my life. . . . It's all-consuming." Another principal said, "This isn't a job [for the social justice leader], this is a life. . . . It's not something I can leave when I leave this place; it encompasses me. It fully encompasses my whole life. . . . This is my life." The principals typified that personal nature of the social justice leader. They shared a deep connection to the positions and to their schools. One principal stated, "I live and breathe the school."

I am not arguing that all passionate leaders who work extremely long hours are social justice leaders. This is not the one defining characteristic of social justice principals. There are many principals who have a zest for their position, their school, and improving their educational environment who also work day and night. However, this personal, passionate, and visionary nature helps to make social justice leaders successful.

The leaders felt a personal connection to their schools and to social justice and can translate that into seeing a better way. It was that personal vision that allowed them to focus their efforts and the work of their staff in achieving equity and social justice for marginalized students. This passion came across as sincerity, and while the principals encountered tremendous resistance, their sincerity and personal connection to the school and their children was recognized and respected by allies and resistors. This passion, vision, and personal nature also added to the struggle, the discouragement, and the toll. They were tightly connected to their work and their schools. The issues and problems felt personal, and when they could not change things or could not change things fast enough, that feeling of dissatisfaction became their inner turmoil.

Tenacious Commitment to Justice

The leaders maintained a fierce commitment to their vision of social justice. The working definition of this tenacious commitment is that these principals sustained a steady and persistent focus on equity and justice for their staff as well as for themselves. Scheurich and Skrla (2003) describe this as "learning to believe the dream is possible" (p. 9); Rapp (2002) illustrates this tenacious commitment with an image of the "1989 photo of the Chinese dissident before the tank in Tiananmen Square" (p. 236). While they may share some characteristics with other leaders, their ability to see a better and more just way (Theoharis & Causton-Theoharis, 2008), maintain a course in getting there in the face of looming barriers, and lead people around them to create richer and more equitable schooling sets them apart from other principals who work hard, who seek school improvement, or who are extremely committed to their schools. In part, what makes these leaders effective is this tenacious commitment to enacting justice.

They described in great detail the barriers they faced as they pursued social justice, as related in Chapter 7. They felt these barriers did not shut down their commitment to their vision of equity and justice. In fact, these principals stressed that they felt their vision remained solidly intact. "I don't think the core feeling behind [my vision and ideals] has really changed. . . . I don't think they've extinguished the internal fire at all," commented Principal Natalie.

Principal Taylor, in responding to the question of whether her vision or passion had changed, said, "I don't think so, I don't think so! And I didn't hesitate to say that."

Two other principals felt that through their experience and the resistance they faced, they felt a greater commitment to their vision about social justice. Principal Tracy noted,

> I became even more resolved in what I believed . . . that this is what's right and it's possible. It's not only what's right in the abstract, it can happen and in fact it does happen when we really believe in it.

Principal Eli discussed how he felt in response to the continual resistance he faced: "[The resistance] makes me tougher, stronger, more dedicated to having success. . . . It makes me feel like I want to do even more . . . like I don't want to give up."

In working against the unjust norms of schooling, the principals maintained a tenacious commitment to their vision of social justice. For many, having even small successes fueled their commitment and helped cement their vision. For some, the resistance they faced made them even more resolute in their ideals and beliefs about equity in schools. This unwavering commitment to their own vision would imply that these leaders are autocratic and lead in a very top-down manner. This is far from the truth.

While they set the course for their schools in terms of social justice and equity, they led in collaborative, democratic, and empowering ways. They did not impose curriculum or practices; they relied on staff, supported teachers, and facilitated schoolwide shared decision making. They blended headstrong commitment to their vision with a strong belief in empowering and trusting teachers while simultaneously building staff leadership that created a dynamic school atmosphere and environment. This is clearly distinct from schools where the principal is autocratic and imposes decisions in a top-down manner. It is equally distinct from schools where committees and the entire staff discuss the direction and priorities of the school, in what one principal referred to as style of decision making of "holding hands, singing 'Kum ba ya,' namby-pamby, everyone on staff feels good, but the needy kids are not at the center."

While enacting social justice in the face of resistance, they adopted a leadership style that embodies a hybrid of democratic leadership and principal-driven change. This style resonates with the leadership that Capper, Theoharis, and Keyes (1998) described as necessary to implement and sustain inclusive schooling. They depicted leaders who set the course for making their school inclusive for students with disabilities but decided collaboratively with staff on how to accomplish that task. The principals leading for social justice in this book follow a similar pattern. They decided the direction of the school in terms of enacting equity changes, but they relied on their staff's professional knowledge to decide on how to best reach that set destination. This combination of headstrong persistence to their agenda of social justice with an empowerment of those they work with creates a complex and dynamic leadership style.

In sum, to better understand social justice leadership, it is necessary to come to grips with the notion that social justice leadership is not a job someone does from a distance, not a position for which a principal punches in and punches out. This work, with all the bold possibilities and all the turmoil, requires a grounding in social justice and a complex, highly intelligent, passionate, personal, and humble leader.

CONCLUSION

The leadership traits and this broad consciousness/knowledge/skill base were central to these principals' work and identity as a school leader. The resulting combination of the three traits with this consciousness/knowledge/skill base coming together within each of these principals allowed them to "see a better way," commit themselves to more equitable practices, and help bring school staff and families with them in moving in the direction of social justice. This leadership moves beyond present-day definitions of good leadership, to be discussed in the final chapter. They demonstrate, according to one principal, that

> what is right is also what is possible. It's not only what's right in the abstract; it can happen and in fact it does happen when we really believe in it, when we understand the intricacies and the details of equity and justice in schools. When we deeply commit ourselves to this, when it is woven into our lives, that's where we see results. That's where we find promise.

"But That's Just Good Leadership": Lessons and Directions for Social Justice Leadership

It is today we must create the world of the future.

—Eleanor Roosevelt

Come to the edge.
We might fall.
Come to the edge.
It's too high.
COME TO THE EDGE!
And they came,
And he pushed,
and they flew.
—Christopher Logue, "Come to the Edge"

THE PRINCIPALS, in their work in SJL, accomplished significant steps while facing overwhelming barriers. It is potentially easy to see these leaders as heroes, larger than life, working at idyllic schools. This is far from the truth. One of the most powerful lessons I took away from this group was that while they achieved impressive changes for marginalized students, the principals were normal, everyday people doing regular everyday work—however different their approach. Their schools, which saw significant positive changes, were not utopia. In many ways these schools with triumphs and struggles, great teachers and regular ones, community and dissent, faced the same issues as every other school and were never perfect places.

However, this framework for SJL provides a way to conceptualize boundary-pushing ideas of school leadership. The framework begins with the social justice leader as the center. The social justice leader both recognizes and works to change the injustice present at the school. This involves creating more just and equitable schools by increasing access to the core learning context, improving the teaching and curriculum, and creating a climate of belonging. In doing this, the leader encounters numerous barriers. While facing these barriers, the leader develops resilience to sustain the work to advance justice and equity. Coming from this framework and the seven keys to SJL, this concluding chapter articulates a series of lessons salient for educators involved in both leadership practice and preparation that leads to the distinction between the traditional notion of "good" leadership and SJL.

LESSONS FOR EDUCATORS

The work of the seven principals cannot be boiled down to a checklist for current and future leaders; however, there are a series of lessons to be learned when considering operationalizing the ideas and practices of SJL. The list of seven keys in Chapter 1 is reiterated below to ground this discussion and frame these lessons.

Key 1. Acquire broad, reconceptualized consciousness/knowledge/skill base.
Key 2. Possess core leadership traits.
Key 3. Advance inclusion, access, and opportunity for all.
Key 4. Improve the core learning context—both the teaching and the curriculum.
Key 5. Create a climate of belonging.
Key 6. Raise student achievement.
Key 7. Sustain oneself professionally and personally.

Operationalizing Keys 1 and 2: Belief, Skills, and Will

Believe in the Dream: Equity and Social Justice Are Possible. The first lesson from these principals is the importance of believing that equity is possible. The leaders featured here and the advancements they led provide evidence and concrete examples that social justice in schools is more than rhetoric; indeed it *can* be achieved. This viewpoint counters the liberal dogma that society's failings and poverty are too overwhelming for schools to educate all students to a similar level. In addition, it counters the conservative mantra that public schools are failing underserved populations and that programs that offer vouchers, rely on competitive market-based structures, or induce sanctions are needed to fix schools and counters the view of some administrators that equity and justice are really not possible. The belief that equity was possible was, as one principal described it, "a sense of never being satisfied" and a "deep commitment to always looking to improve." This positioned the socially just school not as a static target that was ultimately achieved, but as one other principal featured in this book saw it—"a belief that we can do better for our marginalized students, changing the present-day realities to move there, and a constant effort to recognize that we must always reexamine our progress." Examples of the successes of the principals provide important models of what can happen in schools for marginalized students and the need to be restless with present-day accomplishments, grounding social justice not in theoretical terms but in actual schools with real-life leaders.

Through analysis of the leaders' experiences, it is clear that advancing social justice is difficult, painful, and physically and emotionally depleting. The data also clearly supports that increasing inclusion and access, improving the core learning context, creating a climate of belonging, and raising student achievement is possible. Believing the alternative—that disparate achievement and continued marginalization are certainties—will only relegate increasing numbers of children to the back of the education bus.

Develop Skills and Will for Social Justice Leadership. Although the leaders described here represent a small group of principals from a small number of urban schools, they provide good examples of real possibilities for improving the education of our most marginalized students. They held on to the idealism that social justice in schools is a necessary, ongoing struggle, and with that idealism they achieved results. Their ability to find ways to meet individual needs in an inclusive, community-oriented manner and their commitment to access for all students and insistence on quality and breadth in programs redefine leadership. Their work to improve the quality of the teaching staff, while placing tremendous trust and power in the hands of the professionals at their schools, offers a refreshing model for others. Their ability to connect with diverse students, staff, families, and community members was perhaps central to the personalities of these six principals, and also a mark of their beliefs about community.

Given that the leaders possessed much of their social justice consciousness, knowledge, and skills required for justice and equity work prior to their formal principal preparation program, can this social justice leadership be taught? For two reasons, I need to believe that the answer to this question is yes. First, it is too dangerous an assumption that the only way to achieve social justice in schools is by recruiting people with a passion for social justice to do this work. It is imperative to reject the hero myth of leadership (Loewen, 2008; Murphy, 2007), which can lead to the false belief that only a small group of leaders can bring about social justice. Second, the principals possessed a particular drive, knowledge, and set of skills that they brought to the position, and they learned that at various points in their lives on their paths to administration. It is indeed possible to teach future administrators to understand the breadth of knowledge and skills, and it is also possible to light a spark or develop a consciousness in someone to see that advancing equity and justice must be central to school administration.

Social justice leadership in schools will only happen when as a field and as a nation we commit ourselves to alternative forms of seeking out and recruiting future leaders with the consciousness and abilities to carry out an equity agenda and we create preparation programs to facilitate the development of the necessary social justice consciousness, knowledge, and skills required of social justice leaders, as described in Chapter 9.

Operationalizing Key 6: Raising Student Achievement by Engaging in a Three-Legged Approach to School Improvement

The work of the leaders to engage in comprehensive improvements centered on issues of equity and justice, and the resulting achievement gains they experienced suggests that the three-legged approach to school reform is worthy of consideration as another lesson for future and current school leaders. As discussed in Chapter 6, this three-legged approach increased inclusion and access to an improving/improved core learning context while building a climate of belonging. This was done to create a more just and equitable school that raised student achievement.

Operationalize Key 3: Increase Inclusion, Access, and Opportunity. Essential to the three-legged approach involved in the work of these principals and SJL is that inclusive schooling is a necessary and enriching component for enacting justice. The principals provided thoughtful examples of how every student (students with disabilities; ELL students; students of varying racial, socioeconomic, and cultural backgrounds) can and must be included in a rigorous and engaging general curriculum. They concluded that not only is inclusion a moral issue, but also a collaboratively planned, differentiated curriculum and instruction can meet all students' needs when carried out in warm and welcoming schools and classrooms.

This is a key lesson as schools across the country maintain structures that isolate, track, and segregate instead of structuring inclusion and belonging. The notion of SJL presented here and the work of the principals directly contradicted many current practices and reforms that propose that the best ways for students with disabilities, students learning English, and other struggling students to learn involves individually designed or remedial instruction conducted outside the general classroom.

Operationalize Key 4: Improve the Core Learning Context—A Social Justice Instructional Leadership Stance. The second aspect of the three-legged approach to school improvement is improving the core learning context—both the teaching and curriculum. In order to enact social justice in public schools, combining an equity lens with staff development, hiring, and supervision was effective at increasing staff capacity to carry out a comprehensive schoolwide agenda focused on equity and justice. The importance of staff development and professional learning is not new, but a focused plan where all learning ties to larger equity and justice issues is far from the reality in many schools and districts.

Related to this is a commitment to trusting and empowering staff. The principals provided vibrant examples of dynamic leadership relentlessly committed to their vision of justice and equity. They held high expectations for their staff to ensure equity, without micromanaging. The leaders trusted, gave responsibility, and relied on the professional decision-making power of their teachers. In combination these implications call for leaders to embody the complicated mix of a passionate, resolved commitment to a social justice vision with sincere humility. This leadership mix simultaneously weaves a determined message of equity and justice into all aspects of the school, humbly admits mistakes, and relies on the professional judgment of others. This almost paradoxical style of leadership brings in what scholars and practitioners have argued for years about the power of visionary leadership and the impact of democracy in practice.

Operationalize Key 5: Build a Climate of Belonging. The final aspect of the three-legged approach to school reform is building a climate of belonging. This involves setting a tone and creating a climate that deeply respects and values the racial, cultural, and economic diversity represented in many public schools. Building this school tone and climate requires an ongoing commitment to building relationships between students, between staff members, and family by family. This only happens by understanding (not judging) families' lives/beliefs; by committing to reach out and listen to families; and by using persistent, diverse, and native language communication. The leaders additionally incorporated classroom community building, a welcoming school atmosphere, specific outreach to historically disconnected families, social responsibility as part of the curriculum, and community partnerships as ways to enhance this climate of belonging. This key lesson challenges the growing trend wherein schools are so focused on preparing students to pass tests that learning and the entire school experience has become void of enjoyment for staff and students.

Reducing Barriers and Rethinking Support for SJL

SJL at the school level requires future and current district administrators to have the ability and will to focus their districtwide vision on enacting social justice. The principals found continual resistance from their supervisors, other central office administrators, and the district structure/bureaucracy. The principals called for district administrators to commit to and support social justice work in the schools and for preparation programs to prepare future district administrators in this manner. That commitment involved seeking leaders capable of enacting this rigorous agenda. Additionally, this commitment requires district administrators to be open to nontraditional leadership qualities (Rapp, 2002; Scheurich, 1998; Theoharis, 2007) that provide an alternative to the metanarrative of school leadership that has for so long resulted in disparate achievement.

Reducing barriers involves district-level administrators engaging in professional learning and reflection around issues of equity, diversity, and social justice. Along with that, reducing the barriers means that as budgets get tighter it is necessary to not put more and greater responsibility on the principal. It also requires creating time and opportunities for principals to gather together to support each other and learn together around issues of equity.

Additionally, this involves an appeal to forces beyond district control. In this time of high-stakes evaluations and dwindling resources, these social justice principals reported that they were expected to do more and more with fewer resources. Educators and policy makers need to find ways to not continually add to the responsibilities of principals, as they are necessary and central to school change and schools and leading more socially just organizations.

Scheurich and Skrla (2003) stated that leaders committed to equity and justice are advancing their vision under "nearly impossible" circumstances. The current realities of school leadership and the experiences of these principals raise two questions: When more responsibility is continually added to principals' duties, with fewer resources, when will "nearly impossible" become "actually impossible"? When will the job and responsibilities in the face of resistance become so great that it will no longer be remotely feasible to enact justice?

Operationalizing Key 7: Developing Resilience

It is irresponsible to prepare leaders to take on enormous challenges and face serious barriers without an understanding of how to sustain oneself professionally and personally. Certainly, particular knowledge, skills, and dispositions are needed for SJL. However, often overlooked components of this knowledge and skills are the resistance that principals will face in seeking justice and equity and how they can develop their own strategies to effectively deal with that formidable resistance. It is imperative to prepare leaders not only who can believe in more just schooling, but also who are capable of enacting this vision without martyring themselves in the process. SJL is dependent not only on a belief and vision of equity, not only on initiating equity-oriented changes, but also on the ability to sustain this work and sustain oneself in the process.

In order to sustain this social justice work, current and future administrators need to develop resilience that involves rejecting the dangerous ideology of individualism that purports that people acting on their own accord are responsible for themselves and for change. While the principals were very capable leaders in their communities, a primary strategy in sustaining their SJL was seeking out and building networks of support. This involved school-level structures, small groups of supportive administrators, and family/community outside of school.

A second means of developing resilience requires that current and future principals develop self-care strategies (like the ones described in Chapter 8) and share them with their supportive network. While this recommendation may appear to some to be overly "touchy-feely," the principals described here unanimously relied on these strategies to sustain themselves in furthering their social justice agenda in the face of harsh resistance.

All 7 Keys Together: Seeing the Interconnected Nature of SJL

SJL means that each decision, every aspect of the principalship described here, and all details of the school are examined and seen from a social justice perspective. Transforming a school is not *only* about implementing a particular reform or making the school more inclusive or participating in professional learning in mathematics; each interaction—each decision—becomes about enacting justice. All aspects of the school, from the schedule to supervision to professional development to family relations, are no longer distinct but interrelate in creating a just school. Indeed, it is the interrelation that wears on the social justice leader, because decisions are never about only one thing. They are never just contained to the playground, after-school programs, transportation, passing time, the schedule, attendance, literacy materials, hiring, safety, teaching teams, curriculum, class placement, or specific room usage. The social justice leader sees and feels the connection between these issues and the principles of justice that undergird them. Principal Tracy described this:

> When a Latino boy is sent to the office for being disruptive before school, not only is the impact on me the actual time it takes to solve the particular discipline issue, but also I immediately struggle with why Tomas, this Latino boy, is in trouble and why other students were not sent to the office. I wonder and later know that the incident involving this particular student happened because Tomas did not have a permission slip for a particular after-school program. The slip needed to be turned in that day, and there are transportation issues with his family, which meant a family member could not come to school with the permission slip. I felt this huge tension because the only thing this boy was looking forward to that day and perhaps that month was this after-school program and working with the after-school staff. I wonder and ask questions about whether there was adequate [culturally and linguistically responsive] communication with the boy's family about this after-school program and the permission slip. Did an interpreter call? We have Spanish- [and] English-language permis-

sion slips. Did an English-only permission slip go home? I struggle with the fact that because this student was sent to the office, not only did the child miss breakfast and will go hungry until lunch, but parents and other students saw this Latino boy sitting in the office for getting in trouble. This public sighting not only negatively labels this child as a troublemaker, but it also reinforces negative stereotypes for families passing the office about this child, about Latino students, and about the climate and nature of our school. I feel caught in the tension between the institutional racism that lowers behavioral expectations for students of color and the institutional racism that labels students of color behavior as deviant and severely and frequently punishes for this behavior. In terms of leadership, I immediately feel the weight of all of those issues from just one incident. Understanding that this "discipline" incident was not truly about a child being disruptive but about a series of justice-embedded issues, I feel the need and responsibility to address the justice concerns at the heart of it. This is much harder than talking to Tomas about behavior. These are huge issues. . . . these things weigh so heavily upon me.

Principal Tracy felt responsible for the injustices he saw in this situation. He clearly articulated this interconnected nature of SJL and the ways a single incident, seen from a justice angle, can reflect a host of interrelated power questions and ramifications. When he shared this story about Tomas with the other principals, it became clear that they, too, did not see this as a simple disciplinary issue, were passionate about the broader context this situation arose from and affected, and maintained a fierce commitment toward what they saw as socially just or unjust ways to handle situations. Ultimately, this boy made amends to the other student and staff member involved in the before-school altercation. More important, the interpreter and Principal Tracy took this young man home to discuss the after-school program (not the discipline situation) with his family. This was a family Principal Tracy had not deeply connected with until this situation. He learned that this boy was expected to walk younger siblings, cousins, and neighbors home after school, and the family was relying on his leadership 1 of the 3 days a week that this particular after-school program ran. A compromise was reached by bending the rules for this situation (all students in this after-school program were required to be there the 3 days each week it was held), and Tomas was allowed to miss 1 day a week. In the end, this boy did consistently participate in the after-school program 2 days a week, and his mother, uncle, or aunt were seen at *every* school event thereafter.

As a kindergarten and elementary teacher for 7 years, Principal Tracy left elementary teaching for the principalship with the idealistic call to have a larger impact on more students. He knew traditional public schools could effectively serve students from marginalized backgrounds, and that conviction brought him out of the classroom and into administration.

As a principal committed to equity and social justice, Principal Tracy loved the possibility this work brought, was nourished by the relationships he built, and was excited by beginning to fulfill the nation's promise—one that all children deserve. But he was wrecked by the pain of being the "boss" responsible for the oppression being inflicted upon students. He found real hope in seeing his convictions come to life in the progress made at his elementary school—progress that nurtured students' potential, supported teachers, and engaged community—but the job almost did him in.

In part, it was a feeling of isolation—without models, without a network, without a sustained administrative conversation on the struggles, interconnection, and intricacies of SJL. The tremendous barriers (attitudes, norms, systems), combined with feeling responsible for the problems (only able to change things so fast), felt isolating, and at times insurmountable, like a 2-ton weight around his neck. As he built his own small networks, he felt what he had never felt before as a principal committed to equity and justice—that he was not alone. There were others (a small but recognizable group) who shared this commitment and valued this struggle.

All seven principals believed in the paramount importance of beginning to fill the void of community, resources, and examples of the interconnected nature of social justice principal work. While seeing these interconnections made their jobs harder in the sense that it weighed heavily upon them, understanding these interconnections was also instrumental in understanding equity and justice implications and maneuvering their systems to continually move their agenda. It was through seeing the interconnections that increasing inclusion and access became more meaningful when that access was provided to an improved core-learning context. And that teaching and curriculum are certainly enhanced within a climate of belonging. It is the ability to see the equity and justice in big and small things and how they interrelate that allows SJL to occur within the already hectic 10-plus-hour workday of school principals.

"BUT THAT'S JUST GOOD LEADERSHIP"

Inspired by Ladson-Billings's (1995) article "But That's Just Good Teaching! The Case for Culturally Relevant Pedagogy," I propose that the leadership described in this book is more than good leadership. In her article Ladson-Billings described that in sharing her work on culturally relevant pedagogy, the usual response she received was, "But that's just good teaching" (p. 159). Ladson-Billings proposed that the historic norm of what is considered good teaching must be reexamined to understand that teaching that does not serve African American students and other students of color well, that it cannot be described or understood as good teaching. She asserted that culturally relevant pedagogy is what good teaching should be and must be made available to all children.

In a similar experience to what Ladson-Billings described, when I first gave talks about these principals and social justice leadership across the country, without fail people would respond, "What you are describing is good leadership," or "These principals typify what the literature on leadership describes as good leaders." I listened but did not agree. In reflecting upon these comments, I have laid out some of the distinctions I see between these social justice leaders and what is traditionally seen as "good leadership" in Table 10.1.

Many differences are articulated in Table 10.1 between "good leadership" and social justice leadership. This is not an attempt to label some leaders as bad leaders (though there certainly are some), but as a way to position leadership on a continuum where even "good" practices need to be questioned and pushed to a more equitable and just level. For example, many "good" leaders rely on professional development as a means of school improvement, while SJL embeds professional learning within collaborative structures and a context trying to make sense of areas of diversity (race, class, gender, disability, language, sexuality) with the three-legged approach to school improvement. This SJL approach is comprehensive, honors the whole child, brings staff expertise together, and takes into account broader issues.

The seven leaders have moved their schools beyond what "good leadership" has been capable of doing. This required reconsidering the metanarrative of good leadership. A democratic and far-reaching debate is a central aspect to changing the metanarrative of good leadership. The ideas proposed here about SJL have come from leaders committed to tenets of democratic leadership themselves; who have demonstrated success with traditionally marginalized students; and who have engaged student, staff, and community voices historically silenced in their schools, thus making their leadership a catalyst for a larger democratic discussion.

Social justice in schools has not happened by chance. It has taken more than what traditionally has been understood as good leadership to achieve greater equity. To be clear, the leadership described in this book goes beyond what has been seen as good leadership and raises the challenge to recast good leadership as leadership for social justice. At this moment in history, leadership that is not focused on and successful at creating more just and equitable schools for marginalized students is indeed not good leadership. Consider that decades of good leadership have created and sanctioned unjust and inequitable schools. Similar to Ladson-Billings's (1995) argument for a redefining of "good teaching," leadership that does not

Table 10.1. Distinctions between a "good" leader and a social justice leader.

"Good" Leader	Social Justice Leader
Works with subpublics to connect with community	Places significant value on diversity and extends cultural respect and understanding of that diversity
Speaks of success for all children	Ends separate and pullout programs that block both emotional and academic success for marginalized children
Supports variety of programs for diverse learners	Strengthens core teaching and curriculum and ensures that diverse students have access to that core
Facilitates professional development in best practice	Embeds that professional development in collaborative structures and a context that tries to make sense of race, class, gender, sexuality, and disability
Builds collective vision of a great school	Knows that a school cannot be great until the students with the greatest struggles are given the same rich academic, extracurricular, and social opportunities as those enjoyed by their more privileged peers
Empowers staff and works collaboratively	Brings a personal vision of every child's being successful, but collaboratively addresses the problems of how to achieve that success
Networks and builds alliances with key stakeholders	Builds and leads coalitions by bringing together various groups of people to further agenda (families, community organizations, staff, students) and seeks out other activist administrators who can and will sustain her/him
Acts as a positive ambassador for the school	Builds a climate in which families, staff, and students belong and feel welcome
Uses data to understand realities of the school	Sees all data through a lens of equity
Understands that children have individual needs	Knows that building community, collaboration, and differentiation are tools for ensuring that all students achieve success together
Engages in school improvement with a variety of stakeholders	Combines structures that promote inclusion and access to improved teaching and curriculum within a climate of belonging
Works long and hard to create a great school	Beyond working hard, becomes intertwined with the school's success and life.

ensure equity and does not create just schools is not good leadership. The kind of leadership that needs to be defined and discussed as good leadership is the leadership the principals in this book have pioneered: leadership centered on inclusion, learning opportunity, and belonging. SJL is indeed what good leadership should be. The SJL described here gives vivid examples of what is possible, what is necessary, and what is good—socially just—leadership.

References

Allington, R. (2001). *What really matters for struggling readers: Designing research based programs.* Longman.

American Educational Research Association (AERA). (2004, April 12–16). *Enhancing the visibility and credibility of educational research.* 2004 Annual Meeting Program, San Diego CA.

American Educational Research Association (AERA). (2005, April 11–15). *Demography and democracy in the era of accountability.* 2005 Annual Meeting Program, Montreal, Canada.

American Educational Research Association (AERA). (2006, April 7–11). *Education research in the public interest.* Annual Meeting Program, San Francisco.

American Educational Research Association (AERA). (2007, April 9–13). *The world of educational quality.* Annual Meeting Program, Chicago.

American Educational Research Association (AERA). (2008, March 21–28). *Research on schools, neighborhoods, and communities.* Annual Meeting Program, New York.

Apple, M. W. (1996). *Cultural politics and education.* New York: Teachers College Press.

Au, K., Carroll, J., & Scheu, J. (1997). *Balanced literacy instruction: A teacher's resource book.* Norwood, MA: Christopher-Gordon.

Ayers, W., Hunt, J. A., & Quinn, T. (Eds.). (1998). *Teaching for social justice.* New York: The New Press and Teachers College Press.

Bell, G. C., Jones, E. B., & Johnson, J. F. (2002). School reform: Equal expectations on an uneven playing field. *Journal of School Leadership, 12*(3), 317–336.

Bogotch, I. (2002). Educational leadership and social justice: Practice into theory. *Journal of School Leadership, 12*(2), 138–156.

Brantlinger, E., Majd-Jabbari, M., & Guskin, S. L. (1996). Self-interest and liberal educational discourse: How ideology works for middle-class mothers. *American Educational Research Journal, 33*(3), 571–597.

Brown, K. M. (2004). Leadership for social justice and equity: Weaving a transformative framework and pedagogy. *Educational Administrative Quarterly, 40*(1), 79–110.

Burns, M. (1999). *Leading the way: Principals and superintendents look at math instruction.* Sausalito, CA: Math Solutions Publications.

Calkins, L. M. (2000). *The art of teaching reading.* White Plains, NY: Allyn and Bacon.

Calkins, L. M. (2003). *The nuts and bolts of teaching writing.* Portsmouth, NH: First Hand/Heinemann.

Cambron-McCabe, N., & McCarthy, M. (2005). Educating school leaders for social justice. *Educational Policy, 19*(1), 201–222.

Capper, C. A., Alston, J. Gause, C. P., Koschoreck, J. W., Lopez, G., Lugg, C. A., & McKenzie, K. (2006). Integrating lesbian/gay/bisexual/transgender topics and their intersections with other areas of difference into leadership preparation curriculum: Practical ideas and strategies. *Journal of School Leadership, 16*(2), 142–157.

Capper, C., Theoharis, G., & Keyes, M. (1998, October/November). *The principal's role in inclusive schools for students with disabilities, empowering and democratic schools, and restructuring schools: A comparative analysis.* Paper presented at the University Council for Education Administration Annual Conference, October 30– November 1, 1998, St. Louis, MO.

Carlson, P., & Stephens, T. (1986). Cultural bias and identification of behaviorally disordered children. *Behavioral Disorders, 11*, 191–198.

Carpenter, L. J. (1992). The influence of examiner knowledge based on diagnostic decision making with language minority children. *Journal of Educational Issues of Language Minority Students, 11*, 139–161.

Carter, S. C. (2000). *No excuses: Lessons from 21 high performing, high-poverty schools.* Washington, DC: Heritage Foundation.

Children's Defense Fund. (2005). *The state of America's children.* Washington DC: Children's Defense Fund.

Cole, A. L., & Knowles, J. G. (2000). *Researching teaching: Exploring teacher development through reflective inquiry.* New York: Allyn & Bacon.

Cole, A. L., & Knowles, J. G. (2001). *Lives in context: The art of life history research.* Walnut Creek: Alta Mira Press.

Cunningham, P., & Allington, R. (1994). *Classrooms that work: They can all read and write.* New York: HarperCollins

Dantley, M. (2002). Uprooting and replacing positivism, the melting pot, multiculturalism, and other impotent notions in education leadership through an African American perspective. *Education and Urban Society, 34*(3), 334–352.

Dantley, M., & Tillman, L. (2006). Social justice and moral transformative leadership. In C. Marshall & M. Olivia (Eds.), *Leadership for social justice: Making revolutions happen* (pp. 16–29). Boston: Pearson.

Darling-Hammond, L. (1999). *Teacher quality and students achievement: A review of state policy evidence.* Seattle, WA: Center for Study of Teaching and Learning.

Darling-Hammond, L., with Eileen Scanlan. (1992). Policy and supervision. In C. D. Glickman (Ed.), *1992 ASCD Yearbook* (pp. 7–27). Alexandria, VA: Association for Supervision and Curriculum Development.

Deal, T. E., & Peterson, K. D. (1999). *Shaping school culture.* San Francisco: Jossey-Bass.

Delpit, L. (1995). *Other people's children.* New York: New Press.

Dews, C. L., & Law, C. L. (Eds.). (1995). *This fine place so far from home: Voices of academics from the working class.* Philadelphia: Temple University Press.

Edmonds, R. (1979). Effective schools for the urban poor. *Educational Leadership, 2,* 15–23.

Ellis, C. (2004). *The ethnographic I: A methodological novel about autoethnography.* Lanham, MD: Alta Mira Press.

Erickson, D. (2004, May 18). Board adds strings fee, hikes fees for sports. *Wisconsin State Journal, 165*(139), A1, A8.

Estes, N. (1994). Learning and caring. *Executive Educator, 16*(1), 28–30.

Ferguson, R. (1998). Teachers' perceptions and expectation and the Black-White test score gap. In C. Jencks & M. Phillips (Eds.), *The Black-White test score gap* (pp. 318–375). Washington, DC: Brookings Institution Press.

Foster, W. (1986). *Paradigms and promises: New approaches to educational administration.* Buffalo, NY: Prometheus Books.

Fountas, I. C., & Pinnell, G. S. (2001). *Guiding readers and writers: Teaching comprehension, genre, and content literacy.* Portsmouth, NH: Heinemann.

Frattura, E., & Capper, C. A. (2007). *Leading for social justice: Transforming schools for all learners.* Thousand Oaks, CA: Corwin Press.

Freire, P. (1990). *Pedagogy of the oppressed.* New York: Continuum.

Fullan, M. (1993). *Change forces.* London: Falmer.

Fullan, M. (2001). *The new meaning of educational change.* New York: Teachers College Press.

Furman, G. C., & Gruenewald, D. A. (2004). Expanding the landscape of social justice: A critical ecological analysis. *Educational Administration Quarterly, 40*(1), 49–78.

Ghosal, S., & Bartlett, C. A. (1995, January/February). Changing the role of top management: Beyond structure to processes. *Harvard Business Review,* pp. 86–96.

Goldfarb, K. P., & Grinberg, J. (2002). Leadership for social justice: Authentic participation in the case of a community center in Caracas, Venezuela. *Journal of School Leadership, 12*(2), 157–173.

Grogan, M. (Ed.). (2002a). Leadership for social justice. [Special issue]. *Journal of School Leadership, 12*(2).

Grogan, M. (Ed.). (2002b). Leadership for social justice, part II. [Special issue]. *Journal of School Leadership, 12*(3).

Hart, A. W., & Bredeson, P. V. (1996). *The principalship: A theory of professional learning and practice.* New York: McGraw-Hill.

Herriott, R. E., & Firestone, W. A. (1984). Two images of schools as organizations: A refinement of elaboration. *Educational Administration Quarterly, 20*(4), 41–57.

Hollins, E. R., & Spencer, K. (1990). Restructuring schools for cultural inclusion: Changing the schooling process for African-American youngsters. *Journal of Education, 172,* 89–100.

Huefner, D. (2000). *Getting comfortable with special education law: A framework for working with children with disabilities.* Norwood, MA: Christopher-Gordon.

IDEA Local Implementation by Local Administrators Project & National Alliance of Black School Educators (2002). *Addressing over-representation of African-American students in special education: The prereferral intervention process, an administrator's guide.* Arlington, VA: Council for Exceptional Children.

Jackson, M. (1995). *At home in the world.* Durham, NC: Duke University.

Karagiannis, A., Stainback, W., & Stainback, S. (1996). Rationale for inclusive schooling. In S. Stainback and W. Stainback (Eds.), *Inclusion: A guide for educators* (pp. 3–16). Baltimore: Paul Brookes.

Keene, E. O., & Zimmerman, S. (2001). *Mosaic of thought: The power of comprehension strategy instruction.* Portsmouth, NH: Heinemann.

Kinney, P. (2003). Leading with less. *Principal, 83*(1), 34–35, 38–39.

Kohn, A. (1998). Only for my kid. *Phi Delta Kappan, 79*(8), 568–577.

Kozol, J. (1991). *Savage inequalities: Children in America's schools.* New York: Crown.

Kozol, J. (1996). *Amazing grace: The lives of children and the conscience of a nation.* New York: Harper Perennial.

Kozol, J. (2000). *Ordinary resurrection: Children in the years of hope.* New York: Crown.

Kozol, J. (2005). *The shame of a nation: Restoring apartheid in American schooling.* New York: Crown.

Kunc, M. (1992). The need to belong: Rediscovering Maslow's Hierarchy of Needs. In R. A. Villa, J. S. Thousand, W. Stainback, & S. Stainback (Eds.), *Restructuring for caring and effective education: An administrative guide to creating heterogeneous schools* (pp. 25–40). Baltimore: Paul H. Brookes.

Kuykendall, C. (1991). *From rage to hope: Strategies for reclaiming Black & Hispanic students.* Bloomington, IN: National Educational Service.

Ladson-Billings, G. (1994). *The dreamkeepers: Successful teachers of African-American children.* San Francisco: Jossey-Bass.

Ladson-Billings, G. (1995). But that's just good teaching! The case for culturally relevant pedagogy. *Theory into Practice, 34*(3), 159–165.

Landsman, J. (2005). *A White teacher talks about race.* Lanham, MD: Scarecrow Education.

Langer, S., & Boris-Schacter, S. (2003). Challenging the image of the American principalship. *Principal, 83*(1), 14–18.

Larson, C., & Murtadha, K. (2002). Leadership for social justice. In J. Murphy (Ed.), *The educational leadership challenge: Redefining leadership for the 21st century* (pp. 134–161). Chicago: University of Chicago Press.

Larson, C. L., & Ovando, C. J. (2001). *The color of bureaucracy: The politics of equity in multicultural school communities.* Belmont, CA: Wadsworth Thomson Learning.

Leithwood, K. (1994, January). Leadership for school restructuring. An invited address to the International Congress for School Effectiveness and Improvement. Melbourne, Australia.

Loewen, J. (2008). *Lies my teacher told me: Everything your American history textbook got wrong.* New York: The New Press.

Lopez, G. R. (2001). The value of hard work: Lessons on parent involvement from an (im)migrant household. *Harvard Educational Review, 71*(3), 416–437.

Lyman, L. L., & Villani, C. J. (2002). The complexity of poverty: A missing component of educational leadership programs. *Journal of School Leadership, 12*(3), 246–280.

MacKinnon, D. (2000). Equity, leadership, and schooling. *Exceptionality Education Canada, 10*(1–2), 5–21.

Manasse, A. L. (1985). Improving conditions for principal effectiveness: Policy implications of research. *Elementary School Journal, 85*(3), 138–162.

Marshall, C. (2004). Social justice challenges to educational administration: Introduction to a special issue. *Educational Administration Quarterly, 40*(1), 5–15.

Marshall, C., & Oliva, M. (2006). *Leaders for social justice: Making revolutions in education.* White Plains, NY: Allyn & Bacon.

Marshall, C., & Ward, M. (2004). "Yes, but . . .": Education leaders discuss social justice. *Journal of School Leadership, 14*(3), 530–563.

Maynes, B., & Sarbit, B. (2000). Schooling children living in poverty: Perspectives on social justice. *Exceptionality Education Canada, 10*(1–2), 37–61.

Meneley, Y., & Young, D. (Eds.) (2005). *Autoethnographies: The anthropology of academic practices.* Toronto, Canada: Broadview Press.

Minow, M. (1990). *Making all the difference: Inclusion, exclusion, and American law.* Ithaca, NY: Cornell University Press.

Moses, R. P., & Cobb, C. E., Jr. (2001). *Radical equations: Civil rights from Mississippi to the Algebra Project.* Boston: Beacon Press.

Murphy, J. P. (2007). The unheroic side of leadership: Notes from the swamp. In *The Jossey-Bass reader on educational leadership* (2nd rev. ed.). San Francisco: Jossey-Bass.

Murray, C., & Clark, R. (1990). Targets of racism. *American School Board Journal, 177*(6), 22–24.

National Center for Educational Statistics. (2005). *Language minority school-age children.* Available online at: http://nces.ed.gov/programs/coe/2005/section1/indicator05.asp (accessed October 5, 2005).

New York State Education Department. (2007). The New York State Report Card: Accountability and Overview Report (2006–07). Office of Information and Reporting Services. Available online at: https://www.nystart.gov/publicweb-external/2007statewideAOR.pdf (accessed August 18, 2008).

Noli, P. (2002–2003). Challenging institutionalized racism in our schools. In G. E. Singleton, *Beyond diversity: A strategy for de-institutionalizing racism and improving student achievement.* San Francisco: Pacific Education Group.

Normore, A. H. (Ed.). (2006). Leadership for learning in the context of social justice: An American perspective [Special issue]. *International Electronic Journal for Leadership in Learning, 10*(19).

Normore, A. H. (Ed.). (2007). Leadership for learning in the context of social justice: An international perspective [Special issue]. *Journal of Educational Administration, 45*(6).

Oakes, J. (1985). *Keeping track: How schools structure inequality.* New Haven, CT: Yale University Press.

Oakes, J., Quartz, K. H., Ryan, S., & Lipton, M. (2000). Becoming good American schools. *Phi Delta Kappan, 81*(8), 568–576.

Ogbu, J. (1987). Variability in minority school performance: A problem in search of an explanation. *Anthropology and Education Quarterly, 18,* 312–336.

Payne, R. K (1998). *A framework for understanding poverty.* Baytown, TX: RFT.

Perry, T., Steele, C. & Hilliard A., III. (2003). *Young, gifted and Black: Promoting high achievement among African-American students.* Boston: Beacon.

Pinnell, G. S., & Fountas, I. C. (1996). *Guided reading: Good first teaching for all children.* Portsmouth, NH: Heinemann.

Pohland, P., & Carlson, L. T. (1993). Program reform in educational administration. *University Council for Educational Administration, 34*(3), 4–9.

Pounder, D., Reitzug, U., & Young, M. (2002). Preparing school leaders for school improvement, social justice, and community. In J. Murphy (Ed.), *The educational leadership challenge: Redefining leadership for the 21st century* (pp. 261–288). Chicago: University of Chicago Press.

Pressley, M., Wharton-McDonald, R., Allington, R., Block, C. C., Morrow, L., Tracey, D., et al. (2001). A study of effective first-grade literacy instruction. *Scientific Studies of Reading, 5*(1), 35–58.

Purpel, D. E. (1989). *The moral and spiritual crisis in education: A curriculum for justice and compassion in education.* New York: Bergin and Garvey.

Rapp, D. (2002). Social justice and the importance of rebellious imaginations. *Journal of School Leadership, 12*(3), 226–245.

Rawls, J. (1971). *A theory of justice.* London: Oxford University Press.

Reese, W. J. (2005). *America's public schools: From the common school to "No Child Left Behind."* Baltimore: Johns Hopkins University Press.

Riester, A. F., Pursch, V., & Skrla, L. (2002). Principals for social justice: Leaders of school success for children from low-income homes. *Journal of School Leadership, 12*(3), 281–304.

Rusch, E. A. (2004). Gender and race in leadership preparation: A constrained discourse. *Educational Administration Quarterly, 40*(1), 16–48.

Sapon-Shevin, M. (2003). Inclusion: A matter of social justice. *Educational Leadership, 61*(2), 25–28

Sapon-Shevin, M. (2007). *Widening the circle: The power of inclusive classrooms.* Boston: Beacon.

Scheurich, J. J. (1998). Highly successful and loving, public elementary schools populated mainly by low-SES children of color: Core beliefs and cultural characteristics. *Urban Education, 33*(4), 451–491.

Scheurich, J., & Skrla, L. (2003). *Leadership for equity and excellence: Creating high achievement classrooms, schools, and districts.* Thousand Oaks, CA: Corwin Press.

Scheurich, J., Skrla, L., & Johnson, J. E. (2000). Thinking carefully about equity and accountability. *Phi Delta Kappan, 82*(4), 293–299.

Schmidt, W. H. (1997). *Third International Mathematics and Science Study.* East Lansing: Michigan State University.

Schmoker, M. (2006). *Results now: How we can achieve unprecedented improvements in teaching and learning.* Alexandria, VA: Association for Supervision and Curriculum Development.

Senna, D. (1998). *Caucasia.* New York: Riverhead Books.

Shields, C. M. (2004). Dialogic leadership for social justice: Overcoming pathologies of silence. *Educational Administration Quarterly, 40*(1), 111–134.

Shields, C. M., Larocque, L. J., & Oberg, S. L. (2002). A dialogue about race and ethnicity in education: Struggling to understand issues in cross-cultural leadership. *Journal of School Leadership, 12*(2), 116–137.

Shoho, A. (Ed.). (2006). The role of social justice in educational administration programs [Special issue]. *Journal of Education Administration.*

Singleton, G. E., & Linton, C. (2006). *Courageous conversations about race: A field guide for achieving equity in schools.* Thousand Oaks, CA: Corwin Press.

Singleton, G. E., & Noli, P. (2001, Spring). Call to action on racism. *Journal of Staff Development, 22*(2), 72–73.

Skrla, L. (2000). Mourning silence: Women superintendents (and a researcher) rethink speaking up and speaking out. *International Journal of Qualitative Studies in Education, 13*(6), 611–628.

Skrla, L., Scheurich, J. J., Garcia, J., & Nolly, G. (2004). Equity audits: A practical leadership tool for developing equitable and excellent schools. *Educational Administration Quarterly, 40*(1), 135–163.

Solomon, R. P. (2002). School leaders and antiracism: Overcoming pedagogical and political obstacles. *Journal of School Leadership, 12*(2), 174–197.

Strachan, J. (1997). *Resistance, agreement, and appropriation: Practicing feminist educational leadership in a "New Right" context.* Paper presented at the general meeting of the American Educational Research Association, Chicago.

Tatum, B. D. (1997). *"Why are all the Black kids sitting together in the cafeteria?" and other conversations about race.* New York: Basic Books.

Taylor, B. M., Pearson, P. D., Clark, K., & Walpole, S. (1999). Beating the odds in teaching all children to read: Lessons from effective school and exemplary teachers. In *Ready Reference for Reading Excellence.* Retrieved September 3, 2008, from http://www.ciera.org/resources/ready-reference/rrsummaryl. Office of Educational Research and Improvement: U.S. Department of Education.

Theoharis, G. T. (2004). *At no small cost: Social justice leaders and their response to resistance.* Unpublished doctoral dissertation. University of Wisconsin, Madison.

Theoharis, G. (2007). Social justice educational leaders and resistance: Toward a theory of social justice leadership. *Educational Administration Quarterly, 43*(2) 228–251.

Theoharis, G. (in press). Woven in deeply: Identity and leadership of urban social justice principals. *Education and Urban Society.*

Theoharis, G., & Causton-Theoharis, J. (2008). Oppressors or emancipators: Critical dispositions for preparing inclusive school leaders. *Equity and Excellence in Education, 41*(2), 230–246.

Thomas, W. P., & Collier, V. (1997). *School effectiveness for language minority students.* NCBE Resource Collection Series, No. 9. National Clearinghouse for Bilingual Education, George Washington University.

Tierney, W. G. (1998). Life history's history: Subjects foretold. *Qualitative Inquiry 4*(1), 40–70.

Tillman, L. C., Brown, K., Campbell Jones, F., & Gonzalez, M. L. (Eds.). (2006). Teaching for transformative leadership for social justice [Special issue]. *Journal of School Leadership, 16*(2).

Touchton, D., & Acker-Hocevar, M. (2001, November). *Using a lens of social justice to reframe principals' interviews from high poverty, low performing schools.* Paper presented at the annual meeting of the University Council for Educational Administration, Cincinnati, OH.

U.S. Department of Education. (2001). *To assure the free appropriate public education of all children with disabilities.* Twenty-third Annual Report to Congress on the Implementation of the Individuals with Disabilities Education Act. Washington D.C.: Author.

Valencia, R. R. (1997). *The evolution of deficit thinking: Educational thought and practice.* London: Falmer.

Vibert, A., & Portelli, J. (2000). School leadership and critical practice in an elementary school. *Exceptionality Education Canada, 10*(1–2), 23–36.

Villa, R., & Thousand, J. (2005). *Creating an inclusive school* (2nd ed.). Alexandria, VA: Association for Supervision and Curriculum Development.

Index

About the Author

GEORGE THEOHARIS is an Assistant Professor of Educational Leadership and Inclusive Elementary Education in the Teaching and Leadership Department at Syracuse University. He has extensive field experience as an urban public school principal and pre-K, kindergarten, and elementary teacher. His interests and research focus on creating schools where marginalized students thrive by addressing issues of equity, justice, diversity, inclusion, leadership, and school reform. He and his wife, Dr. Julie Causton-Theoharis (who is also on the Syracuse University faculty, in inclusive special education), run a school reform effort titled Schools of Promise and a summer institute for school leaders on equity, inclusion, and excellence. His published works has appeared in such journals as *Teachers College Record, Educational Administration Quarterly, The School Administrator, The Journal of School Leadership, The International Journal of Inclusive Education*, and *Equity & Excellence in Education*. He began his career in education after receiving his undergraduate degree from Macalester College in St. Paul, Minnesota. He received his doctorate in educational leadership and policy analysis from the University of Wisconsin–Madison. George lives with Julie and their kids, Ella and Sam, in Fayetteville, New York.